MW00856994

Inside the Hollywood Closet: A Book of Quotes

Boze Hadleigh

Inside the Hollywood Closet: A Book of Quotes© 2020 by Boze Hadleigh

All Rights Reserved.
No part of this book may be reproduced or transmitted in any form or by any means, electronic or mechanical, including photocopying, without permission in writing from the publisher.

For more information contact:

Riverdale Avenue Books
Magnus Books
5676 Riverdale Avenue
Riverdale, NY 10471.

www.riverdaleavebooks.com

Design by www.formatting4U.com

Cover Art by Scott Carpenter

Digital ISBN 9781626015470
Print ISBN: 9781626015487

First Edition February 2020
Portions of this book originally appeared in the 2000 edition of *In or Out: Hollywood Gays and Straights Talk about Themselves and Each Other* published by Barricade Books.

Dedication

As ever, to Ronnie

Table of Contents

Introduction

What a difference two decades make! In 2000 I published *In or Out*, a quote collection focusing on gay Hollywood. At the time, there were few out celebrities, the Hollywood closet was pretty much all-encompassing and legal gay marriage was a pipe dream.

I've since come across such a plethora of interesting, insightful, entertaining and engrossing quotes about today's, yesterday's and tomorrow's Hollywood and what it means to be gay, lesbian or bisexual in show business, that I decided to re-collect them. This collection includes some quotes from *In or Out*, but is primarily comprised of new material.

One reason for this new publication is that a lot of the stars mentioned or quoted in 2000 have largely faded from view and memory. Another is that so many quotes were from heterosexuals, since LGBT+ celebs were more tight-lipped back then. Yet another reason is there's no need to stress what's now common knowledge, i.e., that gay people don't "choose" to be or "become" gay (and can't become "ex-gay") and are not invariably child-less (or child-free) or lonely in old age like so many heterosexuals with absent offspring.

Gathering the myriad quotes that open our eyes and raise our eyebrows, from an exciting variety of sources and behind-the-scenes viewpoints, all into one place was the goal of this project. The concentrated result hopefully presents a juicy yet enlightening overview of what is and what was, peopled by a galaxy of non-clones who each has something to say—and there's plenty to say!

Non-gays in the alleged heartland view gay characters on a screen and hear of openly gay performers and assume gays are now equal to heterosexuals in Hollywood. If only. Also, too many young LGBT+ folk are unaware—thanks partly to mainstream media's avoidance of the subject—how terribly unfair life was back when the phrase "gay rights" was a joke or a hoped-for concept.

Yes, there's still a long way to go, and the threat of fascism in government is obviously not eradicated, but baby, we've come a *very* long way. And if we speak up and stick together, we're *not* going back!

However, it's too often assumed that all is peachy in Tinseltown, that today it's easy to be openly gay and highly successful. Hollywood is more complex than that. If you're not on the screen itself you may have considerable leeway. Unless, say, you direct action movies. If you're a comedian of either gender you can probably be profitably out, and if you're a singer with no plans to act, you can likely be open—unless your specialty is romantic ballads.

If you're selling sex, the required brand is hetero-sex, and most anybody very attractive or mainstream is marketed in a sexual way and expected to live that way. Then there's the double standard. A good-looking female can say she's bi and perhaps not suffer professionally. A hunk doesn't dare reveal a same-sex fantasy, let alone one long-ago homoerotic experience.

Most of the public still doesn't believe in a sexual spectrum—you're either gay or you're "straight," a word whose meanings were designed by straights to be positive, so why buy into that? (the opposite of straight is bent or crooked, not to mention on drugs, alcoholic, dishonest, impure, etc.).

If a movie has a lead gay or lesbian character it's still typically cast with a heterosexual. At least now we have several out directors. Gay-themed films are still very much the exception, though LGBT+ characters increasingly populate the big screen—look at 2019's Oscar nominees. And by now most people have been exposed to same-sex kisses, "even" between males... unlike in 2000 of the Common Era.

A major advance in general and in celebrity journalism in particular is that saying someone is gay is no longer automatic grounds for a lawsuit. Laws don't necessarily reflect fairness, they reflect majority attitudes, and this legal step forward is due to the growing visibility of LGBT+ people that weakens harmful stereotypes and increases social acceptance.

These quotes shedding memorable light on a riveting topic are intended for everyone, straights too—for, who doesn't have a LGBT+ relative, friend, coworker, role model or favorite performer? They hopefully offer fascinating, often surprising background to the younger reader and they update and perhaps astonish, even hearten, the older reader. But what is "younger" and what is "older"? Age and other differences are less pronounced among gay people than among straights, who are more into hierarchies and labeling (and often dissing) differences.

This book stresses that public figures, who for

better or worse are role models, have responsibilities. I've often heard someone ask about a newly outed star, what about X's right to privacy? If you want that much privacy, become an accountant. Besides, knowing someone is gay isn't knowledge of their private life and habits and doesn't strip away their privacy any more than knowing they're left-handed.

The LGBT+ movie star who earns millions per film—enough in a year or two to last their own and their kids' lifetimes, presuming they choose kids—does owe something to truth and integrity and to less fortunate people like them. For one thing, LGBT+ teens still kill themselves at several times the rate of straight teens. Much of that reflects a lack of positive gay role models.

Several of this book's quotes illustrate the selfishness and foolishness of putting money first, before truth, fairness, other people and personal happiness. The out actor is typically deprived of several career opportunities and there's definitely still a lavender ceiling. By contrast, the gay actor who lies and hides behind a girlfriend or wife (and possibly kids) is rewarded professionally, socially, media-wise and otherwise. Which is the more decent—and the happier—individual? The chapter on the closet, *Out and Outing*, sheds ample light.

This book's chapters delve into four sometimes overlapping categories. The core of each is acting... and we are all actors, as whoever penned the Shakespeare plays wrote long ago. Much of life is acting, and as gay or lesbian children growing up in heterosexual households we learn to act early, out of self-preservation. A bigger proportion of us consider becoming professional actors, partly because we're already good at it, partly because it's a paying chance to try on other personalities, also because—so we imagine—it's glamorous and fun.

But acting, for a child or grown-up, should be part-time and a choice. Pretending 24/7 is no way to live, yet most gay Hollywood stars, especially male superstars, are expected to act off-screen too. Too much of the public still expects actors to be, or be very like, what they enact. Images and masks still entrap a big percentage of celebrities. Character actors have an easier if less well-paid time of it; their off-screen lives are rarely as scrutinized as those of stars.

The main point here is that as human beings and, yes, actors—but not 24/7—every LGBT+ individual should be the star of their own life, on their own terms, dwelling in honesty and safety, free from hate, persecution and discrimination, part of a self-loving but not obsessive community of one and a greater community of LGBT+ siblings who band together in mutual support and remain vigilant about ensuring that our human rights remain in place.

Boze Hadleigh
Beverly Hills

Chapter One
Playing the Game

From the start, acting has been considered more or less a game, frowned upon or not. In ancient Greece, where drama was born, the word for actor was the same as for liar. After all, actors pretend, and the words they speak usually aren't their own. Until well into the 20th century actors were generally considered outcasts, immoral, irresponsible; playing rather than working. "Get a real job!" said many a performer's parent. But the game often proves irresistible in terms of attention, and sometimes, money, also providing a chance to wear masks and indulge in emotions. Unfortunately the game may sooner or later exert pressure to conform and pander to the masses in the quest for greater success, adulation and payment. LGBT+ celebs play the game in often surprising ways, yet more and more players manage to combine success with integrity and self-esteem.

"Seem what you should like to be, and the public will be none the wiser."—**Machiavelli**

"There might be a few of them among featured players [supporting actors]… not among big-name actors. No, none like *that*."—movie star **Robert Montgomery**, father of pro-gay Elizabeth Montgomery of *Bewitched*

"Of course I do have gay friends, but that doesn't mean…"—pre-AIDS **Rock Hudson**

"Most gay celebrities spend their time and energy—with publicists as their partners in crime—trying to keep the masses from getting the right idea."—**Truman Capote**

"If the public *knew*, they would hardly believe it. Even the gay public."—**Leisha Hailey** (*The L Word*)

"In Hollywood you can always pretend. That's what publicity's about, and that's why they call it acting."—studio publicist turned novelist (*The Manchurian Candidate*) **Richard Condon**

"It's very cathartic portraying a gay character. On one level, it may be 'just acting.' On another, it's part of being really human—letting out the emotions and the bigger gestures that we're all as males taught to repress in real, non-cinematic life."—**Richard E. Grant**, Oscar-nominated for *Can You Ever Forgive Me?* (its lead, Melissa McCarthy, was also nominated for playing a real-life gay character)

"Now, as we approach 2020, big-screen culture has turned a corner. A huge percentage of the films and performers nominated for Academy Awards revolve around gay and lesbian characters… I think one big reason is we've finally run out of variations on boy-meets-girl."—screenwriter **Alvin Sargent**, who won Oscars for *Julia* and *Ordinary People*

"The boy-girl love story served an economic purpose and to some extent still does... this is non-objectionable unless society employs such representations to mean there should be no other type of love story... Film and television are morally obliged to be inclusive... not just people who look different, but people who don't look to a different gender for love and affection."
—closeted actor/producer **John Houseman** (*The Paper Chase*)

"The deal is this: unless an actor is uptight and insecure, it's fun being straight but playing gay. Whether or not they give you an award. However, I don't think anyone can claim it's fun being gay and playing straight 24/7 and trying to convince the world you're really, really heterosexual."—singer **Phoebe Snow**

"The name of the game is shame: pretending you're not gay. Putting yourself down, and others like you, to please the bigots. Fortunately, the younger you are, the less likely you are to have been brainwashed by shame."—**Neil Patrick Harris**

"To pretend one is another character, temporarily, is fine. That's what actors do. To pretend one does not love or desire the people one does, off the screen, is mercenary and harms many people, given the influence that celebrities have."—Dame **Judi Dench**

"Coming out may be scary, but eventually it's necessary. I don't know from experience, since I never had to come out. I was never 'in.'"—Canadian singer **k.d. lang**

"In Canada if you say we have two famous female singers, one openly gay and one still in the closet, every Canadian knows who you're talking about, even without names. Legally, it's interesting— the closeted one couldn't sue without outing herself."—**Scott Thompson** (*The Kids in the Hall*)

"Older generations grew up with pre-fabricated beliefs and values that they seldom or never questioned. There is no fairness without questioning. Question authority. Question the majority. Question anything and anyone that keeps you from being you and from being happy."—**Ellen DeGeneres**

"The homophobes forget that some of society's children are gay and lesbian. Gays don't come out of pods... People have got to accept and love their gay children. Otherwise what is it all about?"—**Tom Hanks**, who won an Oscar for playing gay in *Philadelphia*

"The parent who rejects his gay child is saying I won't love you unless you are like me and do what I want and act as I want you to act. That is called fascism."—**Sophia Loren**

"What floors me is conservatives who have a gay son or daughter and still oppose [gay] equal rights... like General Colin Powell, Phyllis Schlafly, Sonny Bono and any number of preachers... Such people make money off their anti-gay stands, but how far does love for money or power go with such people?"—**Keith Christopher** (*Another World, Guiding Light*)

"If you don't let us marry each other, we'll marry your daughters, to pass. Homophobes are morons as well as hateful—hate-*full*."—**Boy George**

"I have never come across anyone in whom the moral sense was dominant who was not heartless, cruel, vindictive [and] log-stupid."—**Oscar Wilde**, who in 1895 was sentenced to two years imprisonment at hard labor for homosexual "offenses" (sic)

"After I costarred in the hit movie *My Best Friend's Wedding* with Julia Roberts, Hollywood strongly advised that I marry a woman to boost my career. They're not satisfied if you do a good job on the screen, they want you to act 24 hours a day."—British actor **Rupert Everett**, who directed, wrote and starred in the Oscar Wilde film biography *The Happy Prince*

"Marrying into the opposite sex convinces most of the public you're straight. Cary Grant did it five times. That made him five times more convincing to the average American."—semi-closeted columnist **Liz Smith**

"Marriage can serve as a distraction. Michael Jackson was cleverly deceitful when during the height of his pedophile troubles with boys he went and married Elvis Presley's daughter. Brilliant move!"—Oscar-nominated gay black actor **Paul Winfield** (*Sounder*)

"The big game is making money. In show business that justifies just about everything, including living a very distorted and fearful life. Once you come out, you lose the fear and can relax and be yourself."—**Ellen Page** (*Juno*)

"Money and gossip. The two subjects that fascinate the Hollywood community."—bisexual singer-actor **Sammy Davis Jr.**

"Who's gay, who's cheating, who's got the biggest dicks... the major topics of local gossip."
—former aide to Jack L. Warner turned columnist **Richard Gully**

"As to why so many actors are gay... we learn to act early—almost every gay kid starts pretending he's straight, to pass."—**Dick Sargent**, the second Darrin on TV's *Bewitched*

"Most minorities have the shelter and protection of their families against the outside world of the cold or cruel majority. But gays are a minority within their own family... most runaway and homeless gay and lesbian teens didn't choose to leave home, they were kicked out."—**Florence Henderson** (*The Brady Bunch*)

"I feel very fortunate in that I grew up in a family with three out of four children being gay."—**k.d. lang**

"We all knew that my brother Danny would devote himself to public service. The tip-off came when he was eight and founded a free legal clinic for the dolls he claimed I illegally evicted from my Barbie Dream House."—**Rosie O'Donnell** (openly gay Daniel ran for the New York state senate in 1998)

"Michael Jackson was one of ten children, with a terrifying father. Michael wasn't thrilled to be a boy... he'd rather have been a beautiful white female. He said so more than once. But all that plastic surgery? That's because he was trying to look as unlike his father Joe as possible."—gay black poet **Essex Hemphill**

"Tom Stoppard [the playwright] once said he felt so sorry for me because as a gay man I would never have children... He was under the misapprehension that we cannot, and that there aren't alternative ways to have a child, including the age-old one of adoption."
—Sir **Ian McKellen**

"What's this assumption on most heterosexuals' part that everyone wants to have children? I always thought the best things about being gay were you didn't have to get married or have children and you didn't have to join the army. Then some gays started fighting for the right to do all that!"—**Ron Vawter** (*Silence of the Lambs*)

"I've been called child-less. I'm not. I am child-free. There's a difference. I'm not missing out on anything and no one's forced me into anything."
—**Butterfly McQueen** (*Gone with the Wind*)

"I think having kids has become the dyke national pastime."—**Bea Arthur** (whose two sons were adopted)

"Look at all the heartache Rosie O'Donnell's gone through with some of her adopted kids turning against her. Is it worth it? Perhaps, but I admire Ellen [DeGeneres], who hasn't felt the need or any lack. She and her partner have a great life."—female publicist **Ronnie Chasen**

"A lot of closeted celebs still have or acquire children to pass as straight. Getting married used to be enough to convince the ironically nicknamed heartland that you weren't gay. Today most people with functioning brains know that isn't real proof. But having kids? Maybe."—actor and drag performer **Alexis Arquette**

"Greta Garbo, the most beautiful star in pictures, was horrified when she was asked to play a mother in the sound version of *Anna Karenina*. Yet here she was, a lesbian or bisexual actress who never had a child, and her performance is possibly the best-ever portrait of maternal love."—critic **Boyd McDonald**

"I did know Robert [Reed] was gay. But all of us on *The Brady Bunch* were protective of him... They don't often let actors who are publicly known to be gay play father roles. In spite of the realities of gay actors and other gay men often having kids of their own."—**Florence Henderson**

"When you're an actor you're yourself and someone else at the same time."—gay screenwriter and author **Gavin Lambert**

"I think far more gay kids think about becoming actors or actresses than normal ones. Until reality kicks in. Anyway, from what I hear, in Hollywood they try to weed them out at entry level."—gay theatre producer **Richard Barr** (*Who's Afraid of Virginia Woolf?*)

"Gays and lesbians also go into acting in order to play a variety of roles, try on different masks. You get paid for pretending, then take off the mask and go back to yourself. Unless you're closeted, in which case a mask is on whenever you leave the house."
—**John Hillerman** (*Magnum, P.I.*)

"The irony is, in the old days there were no gay characters upon the screen. There are now, but if it's a major gay role, it's almost invariably enacted by a heterosexual—in Hollywood this is a requirement. So, secretly gay actors still can't do love scenes opposite handsome actors."—Sir **John Gielgud**

"Do I look like a homosexual?"—**Mel Gibson**, who had a smaller box-office than Rock Hudson, for instance

"If I was gay, would I have gained all this weight?"—UK actor **Clement von Franckenstein**, who never married and whose "rock" was his cat Tallulah

"People keep on assuming I'm gay. Every interview, I say I'm bisexual. I guess people don't read much... One thing now, if someone calls me a cocksucker, I right back call him a cuntlicker. Personally, I don't see why either word is considered any kind of an insult."—actor **Andy Dick**

"There's an ultra-right-wing actor, deeply closeted, married and a daddy, possibly celibate now, who deliberately played gay in a movie comedy to further convince the industry and those few of the public who were in the know that he's really actually straight."
—casting director **Lauren Booth**

"Acting is a pretty business. Lots of beautiful people, both genders. With lots of chances and excuses for flirting, being charming, seduction, love scenes… Is it any wonder bisexuality is almost the norm in Hollywood?"—**Robert Guillaume** (*Benson*), whose son died of AIDS

"Bisexual just means you pay for it."—**Rock Hudson** to this author, in an interview printed in *Celluloid Gaze* (originally *Conversations with My Elders*)

"It's funny how most homosexuals and heterosexuals think bisexuality is a sham… Are bisexuals less secure? Are they 'ambiguous'? Does it matter? My question is, how many real bisexuals would there be if there were no homophobia? Hmm?"—blacklisted actor turned acting coach **Jeff Corey**

"Being considered bisexual is just as scary to a male Hollywood star as being thought gay because the average dolt in mid-America thinks it's the same thing… they make no distinction. It's like their ultra-right-wingers who think socialist and communist are the same thing."—Sir **Michael Redgrave**

"In no other industry does a straight get to pretend he's gay. Even temporarily. It's educational for some and a turn-on for others. Of course the game requires them to say in interviews how it was a big stretch and their wives are quite proud of them."
—**Jeffrey Boam**, screenwriter (*Indiana Jones and the Last Crusade*)

"I thought it was excellent that Jerry Seinfeld confessed that when he had to kiss another man for his show it wasn't as awful as he'd previously thought... It's a big advance from when actors like John Wayne compared homosexuality to tuberculosis and men only kissed on the screen in porno movies."—**Bob Smith**, the first openly gay comedian to appear on *The Tonight Show*

"Barbra [Streisand] said her kissing scene with Amy Irving in *Yentl* wasn't so bad... it was 'like kissing an arm.' Thank you, Barbra. I mean, the woman has a gay son, for goodness sake."—publicist **Andrea Jaffe**

"Who could possibly object to doing a love scene with Catherine Deneuve?"—**Susan Sarandon** on her costar in *The Hunger*

"I have played lesbian and had no qualms... Actresses seem more secure about their private lives. Actors are more nervous about gay characters and if they aren't, their handlers' objections sometimes put them off."—**Glenn Close**

11

"Actors are more ambitious than most actresses, and they're given more roles and more years... Some actresses give up their careers, or temporarily, for their families. Actors won't do that. I think that's at the heart of actors refusing controversial roles. The career comes before anything or anyone."—comedian **Catherine O'Hara**

"Will Smith is straight so far as I know, and Denzel Washington is—too much so, but don't ask. Anyway, when Smith was starting out, doing a gay role in *Six Degrees of Separation*, he asks Washington about having to film a same-sex kiss. The older actor says, 'Don't be kissing no man.' Wonderful advice, huh? As a professional and as a supposed role model to younger black men."
—gay black writer **E. Lynn Harris**

"If you act and have been acting for some time, you expect sooner or later to play a gay character. It's routine... what matters is, is the script good? Is the character non-stereotypical? William Hurt won an Oscar for playing stereotypically gay in *Kiss of the Spider Woman*... Yet in Hollywood agents routinely decline gay roles for their actor clients."
—UK actor **John Hurt**, who played gay more than once

"And then there are actors who really are straight, or mostly straight... but if they do drag a lot, like Milton Berle from early TV, or aren't masculine, like Martin Short from *Saturday Night Live*, they're thought to be gay. People judge from stereotypes that are often phony... Did you know most men who wear female undies under their business suits are married heterosexuals?"—comedian **Brody Stevens** (*Hangover*)

"Men who star in dramas, love stories and action pictures are invariably chosen for a he-man image, whether [they're] hetero, homo or bi. Comedians can afford to be more individual and not have to be butchy-butch all the time."—**Robin Williams**

"Extreme masculinity of the John Wayne stripe and extreme femininity of the Dolly Parton stripe are usually acts. Every human being is a mixture of qualities."—psychologist Dr. **Joyce Brothers**

"They do call it acting, you know!"
—**Marjorie Main**, best known as Ma Kettle, reacting to people's surprise when they learned she was child-free

"You play a murderer, people don't suspect you might be one. You play alcoholic, there's a possible suspicion—if you do it well. You play gay, most people will at least wonder."—**Christopher Reeve**, who played gay opposite Michael Caine in *Deathtrap*

"Sam Spiegel was a fat, ugly heterosexual film producer who disliked handsome actors and hated gay ones. So he didn't want Dirk Bogarde as Lawrence of Arabia and he took back the part he'd offered me in *Betrayal*, from Harold Pinter's script, when he found out I was gay."—Sir **Ian McKellen**

"Some of us became directors. Not all wanted to. Some wanted to but didn't get the… approval. The men at the top weren't fond of giving men they disapproved of directorial authority. A few such men got through the ranks... most did not."—gay "golden-age" screenwriter **George Oppenheimer** explaining that most gay screenwriters didn't get promoted to directors

"Look how many Oscars were handed to, say, Billy Wilder, William Wyler, John Ford, etc., and contrast [with] George Cukor, director of so many hits and classics but a one-time winner... for *My Fair Lady*... Irony of ironies, now [in 2004] it seems Ford may have been homophile too. His favorite—or should I say most frequent—leading lady, Maureen O'Hara, outs him in her memoirs... it's not rock-solid evidence. But whatever the truth, Ford's macho reputation does rest on all those westerns."
—**John Hurt** (*The Naked Civil Servant*)

"Oscar Wilde said that bibles and other religious books aren't believed because they're true, they're believed because they've been repeated so often. In the same way, repetition in the media is what conditions most people to accept or reject certain affections or even people."—playwright **Edward Albee** (*Who's Afraid of Virginia Woolf?*)

"We're all bombarded with heterosexual kisses, affection and sex 24 hours a day on TV... How will [same-sex kissing] ever seem normal or ordinary if it's never allowed to be seen?"—**Ellen DeGeneres**

"Most of us never imagine ourselves in the minority position... Say 200 years from now heterosexual activity is mostly banned due to overpopulation, so media depictions of it are frowned on or banned. Seeing women and men kissing would seem as 'weird' as seeing two men kissing seems today… Presentation, or lack of it, is key."—sci-fi author **Ray Bradbury**

"The movie-ratings people pretend their mission is protecting families and children. Bull! They're there to preserve bigotry. A male-female kiss in a movie, no problem. Male/female sex, fine. But one same-sex kiss and it gets a restricted rating so that fewer people get to see it and so it'll make less money."—director **Norman Rene** (*Longtime Companion*)

"The first two mainstream movies to receive an X rating were *Midnight Cowboy* [1969] and *The Killing of Sister George* [1968], merely for their homosexual or lesbian content… Today nobody but the Pope or a terminal Protestant would consider them X-rated material."—Leading Artists agent **Ann Dollard**

"Past practice: *The Oscar*, a 1966 movie, was about a tempestuous campaign for Best Actor. Its source novel included a gay actor among the five men nominated. The movie eliminated him.

"Present practice: *The Loss of a Teardrop Diamond* [2008] inserted unprovoked violence against a gay man in a restroom by the hero, who is never punished or even criticized for the act. That violence was nowhere in the source material by the long-dead Tennessee Williams."—**Jack Larson**, actor (in TV's *Superman*) turned writer

"It ought to be a scandal that *Loss of a Teardrop Diamond*'s screenplay is credited entirely to Tennessee Williams. His story did *not* include the anti-gay violence in this film hypocritically dedicated to Williams's memory.

"Director Jodie Markell is to blame, plus whoever added the hate crime—an uncredited writer?—which she should have vetoed... I'm glad to hear the *Teardrop* DVD has been removed from several public libraries—not by librarians, but by affronted gay viewers. Keep it up!"—anonymous **member of GLAAD**, the Gay & Lesbian Alliance Against Defamation

"The few studies on the subject have linked screen violence against gay characters with real-life homophobic violence. Anti-gay male viewers may feel encouraged to go out and commit acts they've seen on the screen... Some movies sanction violent behavior, and moviemakers are not without a serious responsibility to the gay public. They should be held accountable."
—journalist and gay-bashing victim **Lance Loud**

"Reiteration and familiarity make things and people and habits seem comfortable and acceptable. That's why the media has such a powerful effect. That's why for decades religious fundamentalists got government and media to ban mention and depiction of gay people in any medium."
—novelist **Gavin Lambert** (*Inside Daisy Clover*)

"I just didn't wear any base."—**Tina Louise** (*Gilligan's Island*) on how she prepared to play a lesbian character in a movie

"There were two things I was worried about [doing a gay love scene]. That I couldn't do it and I'd freak out or… that I'd enjoy it. I didn't want to rethink my [hetero]sexuality at this stage. But it was the most enjoyable love scene I've ever done."—UK actor **Jason Flemyng**

"I completely enjoyed it, very much so. Very much so. I don't think you could be human and not be attracted to your same sex."—Oscar-nominated **Elizabeth Shue** on her same-sex love scene in *Leaving Las Vegas*

"When I have to do that scene I'm going to walk over to [David Thewlis] and I'm going to stick my tongue down his fucking throat and I'm going to swerve it around a bit."—**Leonardo DiCaprio** on his *Total Eclipse* love scene

"I'd suck him off."—**Richard Gere**, pre-Hollywood, to *Rolling Stone* about his commitment to playing half of a gay pair onstage in *Bent* (he didn't do the movie version)

"We Brits are less prudish… in the DVD commentary on one of his films, Sacha Baron Cohen, now a big star internationally, says he'd blow some black chap whom he admires —I don't remember who, I was so shocked and pleased he said such a thing for all the world to hear."—**Alec McCowen** (Alfred Hitchcock's *Frenzy*)

"After I came out, I specifically chose to play a real-life raging heterosexual, John Profumo, in *Scandal*. Just to show them."—Sir **Ian McKellen**

"I figured it was about time I got a straight role so I could prove it was possible. I'm okay with it. It doesn't feel odd. It feels like work."—**Wilson Cruz** on playing straight in the $60 million *Supernova*

"Money comes first... I was a teenage star in Disney movies. Then a boy I fooled around with told his mother, who told Walt Disney, who told me I better start liking girls, fast... My option at Disney wasn't renewed, but Walt let me return to the studio to do the final Merlin Jones movie because those were big moneymakers for him."—**Tommy Kirk** (*Old Yeller*)

"If 'hide the sausage' is the straight man's favorite game and preoccupation, then 'hide the queer' is the movie industry's #2 pursuit, after trying to make hit movies."—gay actor turned novelist **Tom Tryon**

"It's a crying shame that whoever now owns *The Brady Bunch* has seen fit to erase Robert Reed—Mr. Brady—from the advertising and promotional visuals for the show because he was gay and it became known that he was gay after he died of AIDS."—openly gay UK actor **Jeremy Sheffield** (*The Wedding Date*)

"The pilot TV movie for the female-cop series *Cagney and Lacey* had brunette costars. One had beautiful blue eyes. But the men in charge of CBS called her 'dykey' and... replaced her with a blonde [Sharon Gless]... Hollywood has a blonde fetish. The men there think blondes are more fun and make them more money."—Australian actress **Judy Davis**

"When I was trying to be a singer my record label, Geffen, wanted me to stay in the closet, and at that time I thought that's what you had to do to be successful."—Cher's then-daughter **Chastity Bono**

"As a singer, Prince often flirted with a bisexual image, which was daring because he really was bisexual. But when he shifted into movies, his vehicle, *Purple Rain*, was homophobic. He went right along with that accepted, mean-spirited method of trying to build oneself into a male movie star. Fortunately he only ever made two flicks."—actor **Louis Zorich** (*Mad About You*), husband of Olympia Dukakis

"*Meet Me in St. Louis* is an all-time classic and a favorite Christmas movie. The leading man, Tom Drake, was young, attractive, charming… and believable as Judy Garland's love interest. He was also gay. The studio found out, then the industry did… they cold-shouldered him. Tom wound up selling cars near the MGM lot."
—**Cesar Romero** (The Joker on TV's *Batman*)

"Over at Metro, Tom Drake and Peter Lawford were having an intense affair. Tom fell in love with Peter, who broke it up and threatened violence if Tom couldn't accept the end. Fast-forward to when Peter was brother-in-law to President Kennedy and had to play it 100-percent straight.

"Post-JFK he went back to occasional male lovers, but not to Tom, who was five years younger than him. By then, Peter wanted them 15 or 20 years younger—like older straights do with girls."
—columnist **Lee Graham**, a friend of Drake

19

"Who it hurts [coming out of the closet] is the actor with leading-man potential. Studios won't top-bill an openly gay actor. Particularly in action movies. Polls indicate that 40 to 60 percent of filmgoers will skip an action movie starring someone gay."—film distributor **Ted Sebahar**

"Another reason male stars are discouraged from coming out is that although homophobia is less and less in Europe, America, Japan, etc., it still thrives in big markets like China and Russia. And Hollywood increasingly has its eye on profits from large Third World markets."—the *Japan Times* English-language daily

"One of my first agents said to me, 'I only want to represent actors who have a chance of being really successful.' Guess he never heard of Rock or Tab or Tony... Then he says, very aggressive, 'Are you gay?' I'm ready for that one. I say, 'No, but thanks anyway.' And I winked at him... This was all years before I came out as bi."—*Dallas* costar **Dack Rambo**

"There's this one L.A. agent who 'tests' for gayness by throwing a cigarette lighter at you all of a sudden. If you catch it, you're straight. If you don't, you're gay... He's known for this!"—actor turned writer **Dale Reynolds**

"If you're truly hetero but seem homo, forget it. For Tinseltown, what counts is 'straight-acting.' You can be gay, just be sure you're straight-acting and can keep a secret. Forever."—singer-activist **Michael Callen**

"This may be apocryphal [but] indicates what things were like. In the '40s a rising actor was outed within the industry by an actress. The press was going to spread the news, albeit in a semi-veiled way. The actor pre-empted the career-destroying publicity by lying to a studio head, who told other studio heads, that the actress made up the story because he'd raped her. Rape was less likely to end his career."—gay historian **Martin Greif**

"It is a system created by hetero males for hetero males… Errol Flynn, after his two rape trials, was more popular than ever. The media and his [corporate and Hollywood] employers knew O.J. Simpson was a wife-beater—it meant nothing to them… The billionaire Jeffrey Epstein, convicted of soliciting prostitution from girls of even 14 [in 2008], still socializes with top politicians and movie stars… In this system, females and gays hardly matter."
—**Maria Schneider** (*Last Tango in Paris*)

On July 6, 2019, Epstein was arrested for sex trafficking of minors.

"Vivien Leigh worked 125 days on *Gone with the Wind* [1939] as Scarlett O'Hara, Clark Gable 71 days. He got $120,000, she got $25,000… *All the Money in the World* [2017] is the movie where Kevin Spacey got replaced after all his scenes were shot. My point is although Mark Wahlberg and Michelle Williams had about equal screen time he got $5 million and she got $625,000, and when they had to do reshoots he was paid an extra $1.5 million compared to her $80 a day. After she spoke up about the gross disparity he donated his mil and a half to charity… You've come a long way, baby?"—openly gay MSNBC host and commentator **Rachel Maddow**

"The 2019 Oscars are historic in that three of the four acting winners won for playing gay or bisexual characters, all based on real people... The best-picture winner is about a gay black pianist and his white bodyguard."—critic **Ron Franzone**

"An interviewer asked me if playing a gay teen on *The War at Home* [TV sitcom] helped me for playing Freddie Mercury. I was... flummoxed, right? It's like asking if playing one straight role helps prepare you for playing another straight role."
—**Rami Malek**, who won a 2019 Best Actor Oscar as Mercury in *Bohemian Rhapsody*

"The queen we would rather see on our postage stamps is not stripped to the waist and wearing spray-on red trousers."—*Daily Mail* columnist **Simon Heffer**, trying to speak for all Britons after the issuance of a postage stamp honoring the memory of Queen front man Freddie Mercury in 1999 (other bigots complained about commemorating a man who was gay and had died of AIDS)

"It's naïve to think because communism ended in Russia that it's now a democracy. It's not, and don't even get me started about Putin... Russia was virulently homophobic before communism, during communism and after communism."—**Elton John**, who in 2019 protested Russian censors scissoring gay material from his film biography *Rocketman*

"I hope for more movies like *Bohemian Rhapsody* and *Rocketman...* about exciting gay singers and musicians... The one had a sad ending, with Freddie Mercury still closeted and dying of AIDS. The other has a happy ending, with Sir Elton John openly gay, happily married to another man and a daddy."
—lesbian film reviewer **Cilla Sturtevant**

"Sean Penn did an excellent job as Harvey Milk in *Milk...* [and] his Oscar acceptance speech, condemning the homophobes, was aces high. But isn't it sad such a film wouldn't have been made starring a gay actor as the gay character? Then it would have been a barely distributed film almost nobody saw."—UK casting director **Ingrid Gibson**

"I'm tired of hearing, almost every time there's a gay-themed movie, that 'It's not about homosexuality, it's about blah-blah-blah.' I never hear a filmmaker or star saying a movie isn't about heterosexuality, it's about blah-blah-blah."—UK director **Peter Hunt** (*On Her Majesty's Secret Service*)

"I remember hearing the new film *I Heart Huckabees* [2004] was very progressive, an entirely new type of film. Well, it opens with a foul-mouthed rant that may or may not be offensive but does offend homosexuals, the only minority filmmaker David O. Russell chose to offend. How progressive."—**Gore Vidal**

"The biggest reason more gay-themed films aren't made is gay moviegoers won't support them. It's that simple. Moviemakers make what the public goes to see. Look at the Latinx minority, now the biggest, 18 percent of the population. But nearly all Latinx-themed movies flopped. People, you've got to go out and support your own!"—Argentine comedian **Consuelo Martin**

"I did a movie, *I Love You, Phillip Morris*, based on an incredible but true story. I played gay and my other half was played by Ewan McGregor. It had comedy, romance, everything… it could have done so much better [at the box office] if half the gay audience had shown up. Like what more do they want?"—**Jim Carrey**

"DVD sales and reaction prove *Making Love* could have been much more popular, although it was far from a flop. It's a moving, beautifully crafted love story… Under-40 female audiences generally love love stories. Males do not… More women would have liked to see this one, with its intriguing triangle and very attractive cast of Kate Jackson and two 'hunk' actors.

"What happened was, younger women gave their boyfriends or husbands the power of veto. They went to see what *he* wanted… Then and now I say, Ladies, go alone. Go with a girlfriend. Take your parents. But go see what *you* want to see. And at least make him compromise now and then."—**Arthur Hiller**, the 1982 film's director

"In the arts, be it writers or actors, gay men feuding with each other are as common as saline implants in the waiting rooms of casting directors' offices."—**Truman Capote**, who had a decades-long feud with fellow gay author Gore Vidal

"I know two top casting directors that can make you a star if you perform certain acts to or with them... and it's worse with actresses."—*Family Ties* actor **Scott Valentine**

"My female clients tell me that after years of dealing with male heterosexuals they find lesbian advances a piece of cake."—ICM agent **Eric Shepard**, one of the first openly gay agents.

"How unpleasant can it be for any guy to get a blow job from a gay agent or casting director? But a straight agent or c.d. doesn't limit himself to straight actresses... he doesn't give a damn if you're lesbian and it goes against your nature to please him. But some attractive lesbians are ambitious enough to do so."—anonymous **ex-actress turned line producer**

"The casting couch lives. I mean it never died. Whether it's someone straight or GLB—I almost said BLT—that can hire you... or it's a star with a less stellar performer... not that I've ever been asked, but sex is a commodity in Tinseltown. A very sexual town indeed." —**Jason Alexander** (*Seinfeld*)

"No, no, no, no, no! You do not get to 'choose' to hide under the rainbow."—lesbian comedian **Wanda Sykes** condemning Kevin Spacey's self-serving and belated coming-out after being accused of sexual misconduct with a 14-year-old actor

"Spacey insisted on staying in the closet, didn't give a hang about the gay community, then turns around and seeks shelter in it after a small army of

males makes accusations against him. It's contemptible, conflating pedophilia with being gay. He conveniently came out at the worst possible moment, reinforcing so many anti-gay stereotypes."
—gay filmmaker **Rick McKay**

"Kevin Spacey tried to sound daring when he declared why shouldn't he take his mother to the Academy Awards? He'd never have come out if he hadn't been gang-dragged out by all those lads he allegedly pestered. 'Pestered,' that's a good euphemism."
—casting director **Barbara Dodd Remsen**

"The USA media prefers to closet. I did interviews where I said I was gay and it was all right to print it but they didn't... Then they got actual photos of Kevin Spacey necking with a man in a car but still took him at his word that he was straight. They only like you to be known as gay if you get caught."—**Boy George**

"They were pushing me as an American David Bowie. It worked for him, but I guess that's over there [in the UK]. After I came out and said I was gay the radio people... everyone dropped me... and it's not like I'm supposed to be some romantic leading man. This is rock, glam rock, it's not love ballads."—singer **Jobriath**, who in 1973 became "the first openly gay rock performer," if not rock star

"The powers that be hate that [homosexuality] isn't invisible or mute anymore. But the thing they're most dead-set against is admitting there's any connection between it and romance. Romance, you see, is a potent marketing tool."—**Elizabeth Montgomery** (*Bewitched*), who with costar Dick Sargent served as co-Grand Marshal of West Hollywood's Gay Pride Parade

"The habit is to refer to straight sex as 'lovemaking' and gay sex as sex... The proportion of romance to sex in any given relationship varies with the two individuals involved. You can't say straights are more romantic or gay men or lesbians are. It varies."—**Jennifer Lawrence**

"The network is very careful about any touching or kissing, etc., on the part of Will in *Will and Grace*. Jack too, although he can camp and be witty as an outlet. Certainly *Will and Grace* is progress for American telly. However, it presents Will as what most viewers would like a gay man to be: non-flamboyant, well-mannered and asexual."—UK critic **Ken Ferguson**

"I was very offended, in *Con Air*, that the only character that was ridiculed was the gay guy."
—**Rosie O'Donnell**

"In the long run, the message of *As Good As It Gets* is here's a lonely, pathetic victim homo who at the end finds happiness because he learns to draw naked women. What a horrible message!"—playwright **Harvey Fierstein** (*Torch Song Trilogy*)

"It's understandable why most American actors won't essay homosexual roles. They're all villains and victims... underwritten and under-sympathized."
—**Peter Finch**, who won two British Oscars for playing gay

"We all expect to play a homosexual character. At the very least once."—UK star actor **Daniel Day-Lewis**

"I was given this semi, crypto, secretly queer character to do [on TV's *Love, American Style*]. The director said it was written in a hurry. 'You'll have to bring your own intangibles with you,' he said. I wasn't sure what he meant till I realized he didn't mean those little orange fruits."—camp icon **Paul Lynde**

"After I did *Making Love* most Hollywood producers just wouldn't believe I wasn't gay. If I went out with a girl, many of them would figure it was a camouflage."—**Harry Hamlin** (*L.A. Law*)

"The worst thing that's happened to gay and lesbian actors is video cameras... and videorazzi. Once you're out of the confines of your home, even in your own backyard, and of course out shopping, walking, anything, they can film you and your partner and sell it to *Hard Copy* or whomever.

"And if you're openly gay like Ellen and her girlfriend Anne [Heche] they'll try and provoke you into photogenic rage by making homophobic comments."
—"concierge to the stars" **James Maderitz** of the Registry Hotel, Newport Beach, California

"If you say someone gay and famous is gay you'll often be challenged with 'Prove it.' It's nearly impossible, short of photographic evidence, to prove anybody's sexuality. So the thing to do is answer back, 'Prove he isn't. Prove he's heterosexual.'"—Trans radio/TV talk show host **Connie Norman**

"A neighbor of mine told a friend Katharine Hepburn was actually straight. I was there, so I asked, 'What do you base that on?' She said she saw *The Aviator*, about Howard Hughes. It showed Hepburn having an affair with Hughes. I told her I read that [director Martin] Scorsese partly based the film on a Hughes biography by Charles Higham that included Hughes' bisexuality, which the movie left out.

"Furthermore, even if Hepburn did have such an affair, all it meant was she was bisexual. She still, for a fact, preferred women. And what about Hughes' very close relationships—or affairs—with Cary Grant and Randolph Scott? What about all the beautiful actresses he knew who swear he never laid a hand on them? But movies don't show that."—writer/producer **Marvin Jones**

"As with religion, facts be damned—people believe what they prefer to believe. If a given celebrity announces he is straight, and despite the social and financial reasons for him to lie about it, he is usually believed. Look at Liberace—a blind man could tell he was gay!" —UK film critic **Ken Ferguson**

"Movies cost a lot, then or now. You typically get one chance, only... Liberace's TV show was at first more popular than *I Love Lucy*. He was starred in a motion picture, *Sincerely Yours* (1955), where he's in love with not one but two women. An utter flop. Back to Bach."—**Ian Charleson** (*Chariots of Fire*)

"When *Chariots of Fire* (1981) won the Best Picture [Oscar], a viable future in Hollywood opened up for Ian... He was told to 'erase' his homosexuality and any trace of Scottish accent… It didn't work—maybe Ian was too 'soft' a leading man—but he did excellent work in Britain. Though he overall remained in the closet, he did tell friends to reveal the eventual cause of his death. Ian died of AIDS in 1990."—friend **Arthur Melchett**

"Veronica Lake gave up movie stardom because she hated being a product… it was 'like being a puppet,' someone else running her life… We discussed movie stars having to hide their indiscretions and how it was worse for lesbian stars, forced to hide all personal relationships… Veronica was straight but had a gay tomcat. For some reason she called him Thomasina."
—**Allan J. Wilson**, editor of Lake's memoirs

"In the name of the bigger, more profitable straight market or a filmmaker's own homophobia or both, the invisibility game continues. A new [2018] documentary about Maria Callas imagines that nobody is gay in the worlds of music or cinema—not Maria's husband, not any of her directors, friends or escorts. Non-fiction documentaries are still rare."
—music critic **Pietro Cavaluzzi**

"Hollywood never filmed Thomas Mann's story *Death in Venice* because of its theme of an older man admiring a youth, a boy in his teens. Its *platonic* theme. The only interest shown was by a studio that would do it if the boy were changed to a girl… In the end, Luchino Visconti did a splendid job with it. Mr. Visconti is very proud that he has never worked in Hollywood."
—director **George Cukor** (*My Fair Lady*)

"Russell Birdwell was *Gone with the Wind*'s publicist and the man who deflected rumors of an affair between the Duke of Windsor and Jimmy Donahue the Woolworth heir by planting rumors that the *Duchess* of Windsor was having an affair with Jimmy—which nobody who knew Jimmy believed.

"Birdwell also paid an unknown actress to be 'the Lady in Black' who showed up at [Rudolph] Valentino's memorial service each year. The papers lapped it up, it gave the star a straighter image and increased profits on re-releases of Valentino's movies."—William Morris agent **Stan Kamen**

"Not just Hollywood, but the media, controlled by straight men and men passing for straight... they twist everything around. A Hollywood actress drowns. Her husband and a male costar were there. The media goes on automatic pilot: she was having an affair with the costar. Any hint that it might have been the husband and the costar is ruthlessly put down."
—**Jennifer Saunders** (*Absolutely Fabulous*)

"After homosexuality was generally acknowledged, if not approved, there was a longtime fear of including gay characters in movies. Even minor characters. An unrealistic fear. Would anyone at the movies actually walk out 20 minutes into a film because one of the leads has a gay friend or neighbor?"
—director **Arthur Hiller** (*Love Story* and the gay-themed *Making Love*)

"It is deeply offensive when there's no one gay in a movie yet it still includes anti-gay language. At least have the guts to depict somebody gay and then insult him to his face. Why gratuitously insult an entire population? Screenwriters and non-objecting directors are typically to blame."—**James Coco** (*Only When I Laugh*)

"No other group has been as maligned on screen as gays. Sometimes in pictures starring and even produced by stars reputed to be pro-gay. Look at *Beaches*, via Bette Midler's production company. The novel it was based on did not feature the anti-gay slurs uttered by Midler's character as a youth. Who chose to add them and why? And why did Ms. Midler sanction that?"
—**Rupert Everett** (*The Madness of King George*)

"I liked *Gosford Park* except for its gay and non-gay factors. The one gay character is fat and unappealing. Whereas Ivor Novello is an attractive character and was a real-life gay celebrity. Yet there's no mention or indication of any kind in the movie that he's gay. [Director Robert] Altman isn't a homophobe, so why the gay negativity and why the gay omission?"—film historian **Lawrence J. Quirk**

"The same gay-acting man who I'm told is straight wrote *Gosford Park* and the TV series *Downton Abbey*. In the latter, the sole gay character is a villain, and by series' end, when everybody else has been opposite-sex paired off, the lonely gay servant remains the sole gay person in Britain. How timid. How artificial."—TV critic **Gil Howard**

"I was glad Oprah Winfrey appeared on the historic coming-out episode of *Ellen*. Not so glad that

she seems to have passed over the death of her half-brother from AIDS. Yes, one's family is a private matter but she is a public figure and AIDS isn't something to hide. As they say: Silence=Death."
—**Taylor Negron** (*The Last Boy Scout*)

"I finally put acting on the back burner for composing music. I tired of being considered 'soft' and the offers of nothing roles or no roles. The Hollywood preference is harsh men. If you're not butch or angry they cast you as funny goofballs or queer oddballs."
—**Max Showalter** (*Niagara, Bus Stop*)

"That I was a little on the butch side is what kept them from giving me a spin-off series." —actor turned California politician **Sheila Kuehl**, whose Zelda character on *Dobie Gillis* was briefly considered for her own sitcom

"I enjoy buddy movies. But once they became a staple the leading lady's role shrank. The men's friendship and conflicts took up most of the running time and nearly all the dialogue. One buddy had to have a girlfriend, but they could save time by having the other buddy just refer to a girlfriend or wife, without even showing her."—actor turned director **Penny Marshall**

"In many or most pictures the leading actress is there primarily to prove that the hero is heterosexual."
—two-time Oscar winner **Glenda Jackson**

"The rule is, a hero must have a wife or girlfriend, a female love interest. The villain might, might not…

A sure way to make him more of a villain is to insinuate something rather feminine or perverse about him... a mysterious, slinky apartness. Or make him foreign."—screenwriting instructor **Paul Plesser**

"The influence of non-Hollywood pictures is helping American pictures become overall more daring and creative... I much admire our Mexican actor Gael Garcia Bernal for his role in Pedro Almodóvar's *La mala educación* [*Bad Education*]. I don't know which male Hollywood star would consider such a role, even now. But that was a film from Spain."—multi-Oscar-winning director **Alfonso Cuarón** (*Roma*)

"You prostitute yourself as an artist if your pictures never contain anything to make the average spectator uncomfortable... As gay people it's up to us to insert gay characters and themes into motion pictures when it's feasible. Otherwise, nothing will change. For better and for worse, film has tremendous influence."—Oscar-winning director (for *Midnight Cowboy*) **John Schlesinger**

"John [Schlesinger] is English, Jewish and gay, a combination that makes Hollywood executives nervous. He's worked there, both happily and unhappily, successfully and unsuccessfully... usually under closer scrutiny than when he works in England."
—**Joanna Lumley** (*Absolutely Fabulous*)

"Because of *Midnight Cowboy's* success John Schlesinger obtained United Artists' backing for *Sunday, Bloody Sunday*, about a bisexual in love with

34

Glenda Jackson and myself as a Jewish doctor... Wonderful role, which brought an Academy [Award] nomination but not the prize itself, which, in that role, would have been wonderfully revolutionary."
—**Peter Finch**, who won a posthumous Oscar for *Network*

"Katharine Hepburn's four Oscars didn't prove she was a good actress, though she was. However, she wasn't very versatile... She basically got four because she could convincingly portray heterosexual women."—studio executive and producer (*Hunger Games*) **Allison Shearmur**

"If you're admired and you die and you were gay it takes a long time for the media to admit the truth. Like with, say, Katharine Hepburn or Cary Grant. On the other hand, if you're disliked and even if you're alive, even a conservative outlet like the *Wall Street Journal* will out you, as they did with David Gest, Liza Minnelli's fourth husband and I believe her third gay one."—**Ralph Benner**, *Tiger Beat* magazine editor

"People will wonder if one spouse turns out to be gay, is the other one too? Unless it's obvious why they hooked up. Like with Elvis Presley's daughter—she got all that publicity from Miss Michael [Jackson]."
—TV cult figure **Vampira (Maila Nurmi)**

"It's not a big surprise when a woman marries a gay man. Millions around the world do it unknowingly. In Hollywood they usually know... What's curious-making

is when a straight man marries a lesbian. It doesn't happen often. You can understand why."
—**Amber Heard** (*Aquaman*)

"In the old days a studio would marry off a gay star and a lesbian star. That way neither could blackmail the other and one wouldn't demand sex of the other—as some women might with a gay man… One example: Barbara Stanwyck and Robert Taylor."—openly gay actor and Stanwyck costar **Hayden Rorke** (*I Dream of Jeannie*)

"Sometimes the gay man marries a lesbian. Like Rock Hudson, with his gay agent's secretary. The irony is, after that divorce she blackmailed him. And he kept paying her. He could have blackmailed her if she'd been somebody. She was nobody, had nothing to lose. He was Rock Hudson."—Hudson's movie costar **Yvonne De Carlo** (*The Munsters*)

"Profits trump fairness and truth, whether in movies, TV, sometimes books, websites… The Liberace Home Page website was claiming a decade after his death that he died of heart disease and emphysema. In fact he died of AIDS.

"Love doesn't make the world go round, money does."—philanthropist and founder of Falcon Studios **Chuck Holmes**

"Neither Nicole nor I were or ever could be gay."—**Faye Resnick**, friend of Nicole Brown Simpson, who claimed in her book that she'd had an affair with the slain wife of O.J. Simpson

"Older actors used to think they were doing good deeds by closeting their gay colleagues. It still happens. In one workout book—not by Jane Fonda—an actress pretends she and a famous Scientologist were lovers. The daughter of a super-famous singer/actress pretends in her memoir that she and a gay male singer had an affair. Lies, bigotry and greed, oh my!"
—**Rue McClanahan** (*The Golden Girls*)

"Mickey Rooney was on some talk show. The host asked about gay actors. Rooney said back when he was a star there were no gay actors. The host mentioned Cary Grant. Rooney said, 'He's about as gay as my left foot.' Actress Gloria De Haven, sitting next to him, said, 'Mickey, I didn't know you had a gay left foot.'"—former actor **Tommy Kirk** (*The Absent-Minded Professor*)

"Robert Osborn couldn't become an actor, so he became a columnist, then got to host the Turner Classic Movies cable channel. He was gay but ashamed, and willing to closet others. When it comes to being gay, you can't sit on the fence. You're either part of the solution or part of the problem."
—pioneering gay comedian **Bob Smith**

"William Haines, a silent-era star, was caught in bed with a man at the Y. So MGM and the other studios blackballed him... Haines became a top Hollywood interior decorator thanks to female stars he'd befriended. Long, long after Haines is dead, Robert Osborn, the TCM host, announces that Haines voluntarily gave up acting—a total lie. There were letters [of complaint]… so Osborn had to admit his mistake on-air. Don't trust a man in the closet for facts about gay Hollywood."—writer **Digby Diehl**

"Hollywood's most famous gay director, George Cukor, was fired after directing one third of Hollywood's most famous movie, *Gone with the Wind*. All because Clark Gable, when he was a starlet, was the boy-toy of William Haines, a star who helped boost him up the ladder. Cukor was pals with Haines… one day on the GWTW set Gable exploded and said he could no longer work with 'that fairy.' So Cukor was replaced and went uncredited."
—Hollywood historian **Carlos Clarens**

"Director Bryan Singer was replaced on *Bohemian Rhapsody* two weeks before its completion due to protracted absences [he did receive credit]. Allegedly romantically involved with Kevin Spacey while directing him in *The Usual Suspects*, Singer is like Spacey the subject of assorted accusations of sexual impropriety.

"Expect Singer's career to continue, since *Bohemian Rhapsody* is now the top-grossing film drama ever. There's no deodorant like success."
—UK columnist **Colin Protheroe**

"Remember how upset Kevin Spacey got during all those rumors that he'd done a porno flick? I'd have thought he'd be flattered. I don't think anyone would hire him to do a porno, even for free and even back then."
—photographer **Joey Del Valle**, Erik Estrada's brother

"I have never been as proud of my son."—**Richard Dreyfuss**, after his son alleged sexual misconduct on the part of Kevin Spacey (Dreyfuss was later accused of same by more than one female)

"When George Michael was arrested by a handsome undercover cop, record producer David Geffen allegedly advised him to stay in the closet. The advice was money-driven rather than be-true-to-yourself... Michael did the proper thing and 'fessed up."
—Sydney pianist **Vera Cantwell**

"Robert Clary of *Hogan's Heroes* was arrested in the same Beverly Hills john as singer George Michael. Sad, because Clary survived the concentration camps and was in a contractual marriage to a woman he met through closeted gay talk show host Merv Griffin. And Clary wasn't still young and popular, like the singer."
—**Bonnie Tiegel**, senior producer, *Entertainment Tonight*

"I could have more sympathy for a Robert Clary versus a homophobic police force if it weren't for his playing by the tired old rules. In his autobiography he stayed in the closet and claimed his late wife's offspring from her previous marriage as his own. The arrest? What arrest? Gay people? I don't know any that I like. Et cetera."—reviewer **Douglas Whitney**

"Todd Bridges costarred in the sitcom *Diff'rent Strokes*. He has a book out, *Killing Willis*, named after the character he played... Todd is clearly straight and clearly remains deeply shocked and offended that his former manager gave him blow jobs—which he didn't mind at all from his teenage costar and other girls... The book's tone is stereotypically and offensively homophobic."—reviewer **Brian Handler**

"I was devastated to read *Night*, Elie Wiesel's memoir of life and death in a concentration camp. Then came a passage where he refers to camp officials who trafficked in 'children' and were 'homosexuals.' I was appalled... even if he wrote it in the 1950s. This book is in virtually every public library, millions upon millions read it.

"So I wrote in ink in the margin about camp officials who trafficked in little girls and were heterosexuals. If you come across one-sided and anti-gay libel, feel free to correct it, in or out of a library book!"—**Edward X**, a librarian in northern California

"The Establishment wins by divide-and-conquer. It sets minorities against each other so they won't unite to end discrimination. And yet the actual Establishment itself is an actual minority—heterosexual males.

"Heterosexual females and lesbians plus gay males added together comprise 55 to 58 percent of the population. Yet the hetero man rules. Only white hetero male Christians, preferably Protestant, aren't discriminated against, because it's *their* system."
—**J.D. Disalvatore**, female producer of LGBT+ films

"For goodness sake, open your mouths—don't you people get tired of being stepped on?"
—**Bette Midler**

"It's been scientifically known for some time that all humans *in utero* are female for about the first six weeks. But the patriarchy prefers you not know this. Keep males and females as separate as possible, with men fixated on masculinity, 'superior' and in charge."
—**Gilbert Baker**, creator of the Rainbow Flag

"You had Whitney Houston's mother putting down lesbians and Whitney denying… and then Whitney using anti-Jewish words. At least if you're going to hide in the closet, shut up about putting down other minorities!"—**Joan Rivers**

"What's good for the goose: X is widely known in music circles to prefer her own kind but hubby Y is himself on the down-low. So how come she gets all the lavender limelight? Or is it more acceptable to out a she than a he? Just asking."—**FAB! Magazine**

\

"In 1993 Michael Jackson paid $23 million to quickly settle a boy-child molestation lawsuit. Even a tenth of that, $2.3 million, would have indicated something to hide and fear of the truth slipping out. But 23 million? That is sheer desperation and terror. That's knowing that his masturbating in front of boys, urging wine on them and manipulating them—manually, not just psychologically—has to be covered up at all costs."—publicist **Henri Bollinger**

"People don't want facts, they want idols. Even grotesque ones. Michael Jackson was a pedophile. And a complete closet case. And a religious fanatic. And vocally anti-Semitic… lied from A to Z—and those two marriages weren't marriages, and those three children weren't his... But twisted people who don't give a damn about underaged boys or gays or Jews or truth will defend him regardless."—openly gay actor **David Ogden Stiers** (*M*A*S*H*)

"It's the numbers game, Boze. I'm Jewish, Bea Arthur's Jewish, we're playing Italian Americans... The [*Golden Girls*] producers said most Americans don't know a Jewish person. But most Americans know an Italian American and even if they don't, they've eaten pizza or spaghetti."—**Estelle Getty** to this writer in an interview for *The Advocate*

"Yes, producers are money men. They don't want the stars of their projects discussing 'issues.' If you're gay or Jewish and play a gay or Jewish character you might get asked how you're treated, how your people are treated, what are your views on so-and-so. Hollywood doesn't want views. It wants lines outside the movie house. It wants paying customers."—**Paul Newman**

"For years I didn't refer to this, it would be perceived as making waves, and actresses aren't supposed to. But I became a Broadway success and was thrilled to earn raves in *The Diary of Anne Frank*. So is it surprising that I half-expected to get the movie version? But being Jewish, I was not cast as Anne Frank.

"The studio wouldn't want its star to mention anti-Semitism, which by the way is a misnomer. Semitic is a language family, it includes Hebrew and Arabic. People aren't Semitic—that's from the legend about Noah's son Shem founding a separate 'race.' Heaven forbid I should say anything non-commercial in an interview that's meant to get people to pay money to go see a movie I'm in."—**Susan Strasberg** (daughter of Method acting coach Lee Strasberg)

"People make assumptions. I'm fat, so I'm jolly. I'm Italian, so I love to eat—okay, that one's true. I'm fat, so I'm asexual. If I were slim I'm sure I'd get asked about my sexual orientation. But when you're heavy they often assume you don't have one."
—gay actor **James Coco**

"Don't assume gay stars' relatives are more tolerant... relatives of gay people are sometimes the worst."—**Dack Rambo**, referring to Larry Hagman vetoing a lesbian storyline for *Dallas* because Hagman's mother Mary Martin was gay or bi

"Larry [Hagman] disliked his stepfather, a closeted gay man who managed his mother's career... Larry bristled when people mistakenly referred to Richard Halliday as his father."—columnist **Richard Gully**

"Mr. Gully was an Englishman of the old school. He paid a close female relative with beautiful handwriting to write *billets doux* for him that would be found after he died. Those love letters to him from a non-existent female would 'explain' why he remained single after she jilted him—the fiction being that poor devastated Richard never looked at another woman after her."—bisexual British author **Christopher Hitchens**

"Miss Stanwyck has been heartbroken ever since the breakup of her marriage to Robert Taylor and has never looked at another man. She will not remarry."

—closeted publicist **Helen Ferguson**, a close friend and possible lover of Barbara Stanwyck

"It's ironic but so Hollywood that until she finally came out Jodie Foster was closeted by lesbians, starting with her publicist turned manager mother."
—talk-radio host **Lynn Samuels**

"It's so typically USA that polls said your ex [California] governor Jerry Brown couldn't get elected to your Senate because he wasn't married... Your last gay president, James Buchanan in the 19th century, could never be elected today because he was single... We've had a gay prime minister—a single man, still alive—and a female prime minister. I don't know if you've had any female governors yet, let alone a president."—*Monty Python* star **Graham Chapman** (the UK has now had two female heads of state)

"The Reagans were the most outspokenly anti-gay First Couple we ever had. Having their son marry and give up being a dancer was just part of it... Part of their hypocrisy was that when Ron and Nancy wed, back in the oh-so-puritanical 1950s, she was already some months pregnant."—gay comedian turned San Francisco politician **Tom Ammiano**

"Sometimes anti-gay people are naïve or ignorant. Elvis Presley was very close with bisexual actor Nick Adams till he was warned off him. Probably by his manager the Colonel, who was married but known to maintain a staff of handsome young men... I remember Elvis saying he wanted to be

44

another James Dean and as famous as Liberace, whom he met more than once."—singer **Michael Callen**

"Man, if I could ever get people to talk about me the way they talk about Liberace, I would really have it made."—**Elvis Presley** in the 1950s, at the Eagles Nest nightclub

"I never met James Dean, but how I wish I had."—**Elvis Presley**

"Jamie [Dean] and I were very close friends... It was always platonic between us."—**Eartha Kitt**

"After he died, several actresses claimed that they were lovers with James Dean or engaged to him. I did not. I am not so for cheap publicity as to unmake someone else's reality."—Swiss actress **Ursula Andress** (*Dr. No*, *She*)

"Jimmy would never ever have come out of the closet, no. He was far too ambitious."—**Jim Backus** (*Gilligan's Island*), who played Dean's father in *Rebel Without a Cause*

"Insiders expected Rock [Hudson] and Jimmy [Dean] to possibly become amorous behind the scenes... They didn't hit it off. Rock felt Jimmy was surly and unprofessional. Jimmy felt Rock was old-fashioned and coasting on his looks. I loved them both... but Jimmy could have been more polite to Rock than he was."—**Elizabeth Taylor** on her *Giant* costars

"The rumor was widespread that Jack Warner had James Dean killed because Jimmy was threatening to come out of the closet. Jimmy was probably joking, he liked to needle Warner. He hated authority… Warner had a big future planned for Jimmy, and after he died those movies went to actors like Paul Newman and Steve McQueen and made them stars."—**Julie Harris**, Dean's *East of Eden* costar

"[James Dean] was up for a posthumous Oscar for *Giant*, his last movie. But he didn't win, partly because Jack Warner didn't push him in an Oscar campaign. He only wanted to promote living actors who could keep bringing in profits for him."
—**Geraldine Page**, who worked with Dean on stage

"Money drives the engine. If female stars get more leeway in same-sex flirting and ambiguous sexuality, even bisexuality, it owes to their careers being shorter and their not being paid as much. There is less invested in them. The public takes actresses' private lives less seriously.

"The big male star earns much more for the studio, and more often, but can lose them a lot if he doesn't stick to the public's expectations, which are strict and very limiting… The public's wish is the studio's command."—**Sarah Petit**, *Newsweek* editor and cofounder of *Out* magazine

"I e-mailed her after I saw *Trainwreck* and said, '…I guess I should just say it: I'm in love with you.'"—**Jennifer Lawrence** on Amy Schumer, with whom she later worked on a screenplay

"It is the spectator, and not life, that art really mirrors."—**Oscar Wilde** (the average spectator…)

"The *Billy's Hollywood Screen Kiss* ad was shut out of the *San Diego Union Tribune*, the city's only major daily. The management found the widely-published-elsewhere image of two young men *about* to kiss inappropriate for a 'family-oriented' newspaper. The paper did agree to an image showing one man alone."—1998 *Gay & Lesbian Times* item

"Robert Moore, who directed my last picture, often told how no major paper would run the original ad for *The Boys in the Band*. He didn't direct it because Hollywood felt a gay director would make a gay-themed film *too* gay. He had of course directed the very successful stage version in New York.

"The ad had two male headshots. The caption underneath one read, 'Today is Harold's birthday.' The other read, '*This* is his present.' Far too controversial for the early '70s." —playwright **Neil Simon**

"Bobby [Moore] began as an actor. One homosexual character after another—in my film *Tell Me That You Love Me, Junie Moon*, in *The Mary Tyler Moore Show* [as Phyllis's brother who goes on a date with Mary]… He graduated into directing, on stage and then film… No, I don't believe he has clarified about his personal life."—director-producer **Otto Preminger**

"Hollywood is about mass audiences, always has been. When most of the moguls were Jewish, they'd avoid Jewish stories… Today, a gay executive is often the first to decline a gay love story, say. They do this

to show they're not 'biased' or in order to pass for straight. It's a shame as well as a sell-out."
—**Paul Rosenfield** (author of *The Club Rules*)

"There's much said about Hollywood being very Jewish and gay. That's usually at the top levels... and gay among many actors. But crews were and are non-Jewish, blue-collar, not highly educated, not pro-gay. It's improved... they can't be as openly homophobic as in the past, when there were ongoing horror stories that mostly never reached any public or legal level."
—pro-gay screenwriter **Steve Tesich** (*Breaking Away*)

"My lover would pick me up [from work] and other people would make crude jokes about it."
—**Rick Henderson**, prop man at ABC-TV and Los Angeles's Dorothy Chandler Pavilion

"My client, a gay maintenance man, was harassed by coworkers... He often heard things like, 'Get down on your knees, faggot!' And one day he was sent by his supervisor into a supply room that he usually would not have to enter. Inside, in the dark, he was grabbed from behind and shoved into a closet, then stabbed and locked in."—gay attorney **Lee Walker**, specialist in employment law, about a 1984 incident on an ABC-TV lot

"Most movie sets are very straight. Makeup and wardrobe are the only places you see gay people. But half of the gaffers and lighting men suck dick anyway. You should see the glory hole in the men's room at Columbia Studios. Jesus! It's big enough to fit half of your body through."—**Alexis Arquette** (*The Wedding Singer*)

"I have known of casting directors who go to a gay bar or disco one night and the next day at the office or studio they encounter somebody they met there or even took home with them, and act like that other person is a complete stranger or, worse, a strange queer."—**Kenneth Joseph Carlson**, who cofounded the casting agency Carlson-Dowd

"Hollywood agents are tough, grabby and greedy... always trying to compromise their female clients, to emasculate or uncloset their male ones."
—gay producer **Jerry B. Wheeler**

"No names, please. I will say that it's more difficult to know if an actress loves women... There are more homosexual actors than Sapphic actresses. From what I've gleaned, most such women don't yearn for bright lights, makeup, costumes, glamour and make-believe. A homosexual male is often more inclined to find acting and Hollywood appealing."
—longtime Paramount executive **A.C. Lyles**

"I can't remember a single thing I learned in ninth-grade French or Science, but I can still remember how much it cost to fly chili from Chasen's in Beverly Hills to the *Cleopatra* set in Rome for Elizabeth Taylor."—gay author **Paul Monette** (*Borrowed Time*) on Hollywood's influence

"They rarely acknowledge British influence. Americans have no idea how many of their TV shows originated here... their *All in the Family* and *Sanford and Son*... They tried a U.S. version of *Fawlty Towers* with

Bea Arthur that failed. They had more success with *Queer as Folk* but it was watered down compared to ours because U.S. TV has a distaste for realistic gay characters.

"An adaptation of our long-running *Are You Being Served?* never materialized, partly because of Mr. Humphries, the gay character—the U.S. wanted to drop him or turn him black. Couldn't leave him as he was, nor would it occur to them to have him be gay *and* black."—UK casting director **Ingrid Gibson**

"Ken Wahl [her *Jinxed* costar] was incredibly hateful to me... the first time I met him, the first thing he said was, 'I want you to know I hate niggers and faggots!'... I had no idea why he said that, because we had neither of those in our picture."—**Bette Midler**, who assumed all gays were visibly so (Wahl, now an ex actor, was later rewarded with his own TV series, *Wiseguy*)

"[Comedy Central] host Craig Kilborn ridiculed a gay man who'd been called a 'faggot' and had his car defaced because he was gay. Kilborn didn't believe any of this was discrimination and later made degrading and sexist comments about a female executive on his show... After a half-assed apology, not for his homophobia, but his sexism, Kilborn got a big promotion: he left the cable network for CBS and his own talk show, replacing Tom Snyder."—actor **Mart Dayne McChesny** (*Ragtime, Friday the 13th Part II*)

"As long as we have heterosexual males in charge of practically everything—politically, corporately, religiously, etc.—we will endure misogyny and homophobia. Don't count on them to change or evolve. We must change the system by replacing over half of them, because we, women of all sexualities plus gay men, are over half the population."—female producer **J.D. Disalvatore**

"When the rhetoric we read and the hate speech we hear comes from our politicians, media and entertainment, neighbors, families and religious leaders, we internalize the pain in damaging, self-defeating ways. We are wary and afraid to report hate violence. We lose hope as we continue to be victimized. The cruelty, the hate and the words manifest shame."—actor-activist **Ellen Page** in 2019, after Jussie Smollett's bogus claim of being attacked by two white homophobes

"Such false claims as that of Jussie Smollett mislead the general public into thinking there's much less hate violence than is claimed. His alleged self-publicity is reprehensibly selfish and trivializes the very real effects of homophobia inside and especially outside of show business."—Quebec theatre director **Ginette Pierrefonds**

"According to the Centers for Disease Control & Prevention, lesbian, gay and bisexual youth's risk of suicide is almost five times greater than that of their peers… The *American Journal of Public Health* has reported that each moment of anti-LGBTQ verbal or physical abuse raises the chances of self-harm by 2.5 times. Cruel words and laws and beliefs cause real suffering."—the ***Hollywood Reporter*** on February 27, 2019

"Interesting that some of the media has presented openly gay Smollett as a black actor but ignored the homophobia in his alleged claim of violence. The media prefers a black-and-white situation... [but] the actor's father was a Russian Jew. Half of Smollett's heritage is ignored, and his sexual orientation is sometimes shunted aside in favor of the usual racial divide."—actor and blogger **"Simon Love"**

"It's not generally known that you used to be able to sue if someone called you gay... it was slander, it was libel. It's also not well known that as of not too many years ago one can no longer sue for being called gay. That is a major step forward... Each time Liberace sued he automatically won, never mind the truth. He won because of his embarrassment over being called gay and because the society shared his embarrassment." —attorney **Eliezer Fleischman**

"The press only reports part of the truth. I've always been pro-gay [but] people read that I called a carriage driver a 'faggot.' This came about from a shouting match... I'd been to a hearing about restricting New York City's horse-drawn carriages and about animal cruelty... Then this guy's yelling at me, saying, 'Takin' the food out of our fuckin' mouths—and your nigger-lovin' wife too—you fuckin' faggot.'

"So, because of my retarded middle-class upbringing I yelled back, 'Fuck you, faggot.' I later apologized for using that horrible word... and I was due to speak at an AIDS rally later that week but thanks to the incident and the partial reporting, I got disinvited. It made me so sorry that people who believed I was on their side thought me just like everybody else.

"I *am* on their side."—**Alec Baldwin** (whose then-wife Kim Basinger had dated Prince)

"All the sincerity in Hollywood you can stuff in a flea's navel and still have room to conceal four caraway seeds and an agent's heart."—radio star and game-show panelist **Fred Allen**

"It's catch as catch can, luck of the draw. Most actors get a smile from a casting director, even an agent. If you're a gay or lesbian actor and the person interviewing you for a part guesses you are, you can only hope that smile is sincere and remains a smile… Things will get better as older attitudes and people are replaced by new ones."—**Matthew Rushton**, TV, theatre and film producer (*Mrs. Doubtfire*)

"The most important thing in acting is sincerity. If you can fake that, you've got it made."
—**George Burns** (born Nathan Birnbaum)

Chapter Two
Out and Outing

Once upon a time there were no out actors. Not even supporting ones, or the very few stereotypical ones allowed to work in "the industry." There were also, for several decades, no LGBT+ characters on screen, thanks to a conservative censorship code backed by churches, states and intimidated studio heads. The 1960s saw, finally, the rise of women and minorities' opposition to things-as-usual. Decades later, outing was born to expose hypocritical bigots—usually politicians, preachers and sometimes actors—who were secretly gay but publicly anti-gay, who fostered homophobia, enacted anti-gay laws, etc. People have always been fascinated by who's secretly gay in showbiz and rumors, usually true, eventually made their way into print. Many outed celebs initially denied their sexuality but came out later. Others never came out, but today more and more come out voluntarily.

"Don't compromise yourself. You are all you've got."—**Janis Joplin**

"I remember when outing meant a family picnic."—comedian **Rodney Dangerfield**

"If I hear somebody's gay, I don't like them any the less. Unless they make a big production out of denying it."—**Elizabeth Taylor**

"Ever since they found out that Lassie was [played by] a boy, the public has believed the worst about Hollywood."—**Groucho Marx**

"A lot of people have accused Scully [her TV character] of being gay... And all I have to say is this: Thank you!"—**Gillian Anderson** (*The X-Files*) at a gala fundraiser for the L.A. Gay & Lesbian Center

"The real malice isn't in pointing out that someone homosexual is a homosexual, but in pretending that such people don't or—even worse—shouldn't exist."—**Johnny Depp**

"I'm not gay, but I played a gay man."
—**Billy Crystal**, who played one of U.S. TV's first gay characters, on the sitcom *Soap*

"I'm not a straight man, but I play one on television."—**Dan Butler** (*Frasier*)

"There's a young-ish bi actor, handsome, very ambitious, who publicly flirts with bisexuality but who'll never come out as gay or bi... Rumor has it that in his bid for more leading-man parts, to bolster his straight credentials, he's paid a couple of females to publicly claim he behaved inappropriately with them, sexually... I hope this isn't a new trend. But many in Hollywood are just that desperate."—gay activist **Donna Red Wing**

"The rumor is that Jonathan Frid, who played Barnabas Collins on [the cult soap opera] *Dark Shadows*, was paid *not* to come out of the closet... a generous annual stipend, allegedly from Dan Curtis, the show's creator and producer. Barnabas, a vampire, was a romantic sex symbol... Frid's coming out would have hurt sales of the DVDs and other *Dark Shadows* merchandise fans still buy."—*Scarlet Street* magazine publisher **Richard Valley**

"Being honest, open and unafraid depends on several factors. One of the biggest is the era you grew up in. Look at *Frasier*, on TV. Two of the three male leads are gay. The younger one [David Hyde Pierce] eventually came out. The older one [John Mahoney] who plays the father, no."—UK columnist **Colin Protheroe**

"I came out after the torture-murder of Matthew Shepard. It seemed selfish not to do what I could. Since people seem to like me, if they know I'm a gay man that might make it easier for some other gay person."—Broadway star **Nathan Lane**

"You can be selfish and consider all the roles and money you might miss if you come out. Or you can be a decent human being, help yourself and others, and sleep better at night." —**Miley Cyrus**

"Playing a dancer in *Fame* [the film and then TV series] made me famous. But it still limits me in how they cast me... I still can't talk about my private life."—closeted actor **Gene Anthony Ray** (not "can't," "won't")

"Outing is accurate these days. It has to be, or it serves no purpose. In the past, true or not, people might say someone was gay to defame them... There were and still are those who closet somebody who's gay because they don't want him defamed or they're a relative and don't want to be 'implicated.' Or because the somebody isn't stereotypical and the closeter doesn't believe that person could possibly be gay!"
—**Katherine Helmond** (*Soap*)

"I spoke about [being with a woman] because I'd discovered something wonderful and I thought people should know my experience was very real, very normal... I'm not saying I'm gay. I'm just saying I find women attractive sometimes."—**Angelina Jolie**

"Some people couldn't believe it when I said I opened my own garage. I'm good at fixing cars, so? When I was with Angelina [Jolie] there was a lot of prurient interest. I didn't say much about it, and still don't. I am proud of what she said... All I do is go about living my own life."—mechanic-model-actress **Jenny Shimizu**

"People will imagine the most obscene things about gay people's private lives. I don't imagine their intimacies are any more obscene than those of the average couple."—closeted *Dark Shadows* star **Jonathan Frid** (aka vampire Barnabas Collins)
[
"Gay sex can sometimes be as boring as straight sex."—**Anna Paquin**, Oscar-winner for *The Piano*

"Won't you educate us poor ignorant straights? Who's going to inform us about gay people and gay love except gays themselves? Gays need to banish the shame and myths and stand up for themselves... It's post-2000 of the Common Era calendar, time to shed the shame. I know. I'm Jewish but once upon a time out of some shame and some ambition I changed my name."—talk show host **Jon Stewart** (Jonathan Stuart (sic) Leibowitz)

"Go out on a date with the gender you prefer to go out with. You don't have to say anything or make a speech. Sometimes a picture is worth a thousand words."—**Matt Dallas** (*Kyle XY*)

"I was appalled when Trump, the president not elected by the people's vote, kept on criticizing John McCain after McCain died. But I remember being appalled when McCain, during some Republican fundraising speech, made a very homophobic as well as sexist joke. Death does not posthumously make rotten people nice."—hairstylist **Sarah C. Limmer**

"Do you know why Chelsea Clinton is so ugly? Because Janet Reno is her father."
—Senator **John McCain**

"I don't *get* gay Republicans. Why would anyone gay support a party that doesn't want them to have any rights? In fact doesn't want them to exist... Is it masochism, self-hate?... I've read about old-time queers like Noel Coward who were anti 'gay lib' and felt more comfortable in the closet and with all the old discriminations… Pathetic."—**David Forest**, owner of Hollywood male-escort agency Brad's Buddies

"Barney Fag."—what Republican House Majority Leader (1995-2003) **Richard Armey** "accidentally" called gay Democratic Congressman Barney Frank

"The right-wing's favorite tactic against the gay community has long been their claim of wanting to 'protect' children from homosexuality. But not all of our children are heterosexual, and they are the ones who need to be protected… from bullies their own age and the political and religious adult bullies who prefer to hate."—**Patricia Neal** (Oscar winner for *Hud*)

"A friend of mine commented when the guy came into office how Trump is really down on homosexuals. I said, sweetie, he's really down on people, period."—**Cher**

"The first openly lesbian head of a country—the first gay one anywhere—is Iceland's Johanna Siguroardottir [elected in 2009]… Icelandic women's surnames end in –dottir because they're daughters, not sons—as in, say, Karlson, which for a female would be Karldottir. It's fairer and makes more sense."
—**Paula Dell,** stuntwoman and acrobat

"As an Englishman, I'm envious of and proud of Ireland, the nation whose people were decent enough to be the first to vote in marriage equality… and then the first to elect an openly gay man as their national leader [Leo Varadkar in 2017]. No more Irish jokes, *please*."—actor/author **Stephen Fry**

"Actually, Britain has had a gay head of state. Only he wasn't and isn't honest about it… only he belongs to the not-pro-gay party. Or did. I don't know what he does now, if anything. Not that he ever did anything for his own. I know one thing he won't do: sue. If he sued over this, he'd have to reveal the truth. Heaven forfend!"
—gay Australian actor **John Hargreaves**

"We have had a gay president. Yes! But nobody outside politics knew it… James Buchanan the bachelor president was our 15th. He had a boyfriend who was a senator that Andrew Jackson, another president, called 'Miss Nancy.' Indicating that Buchanan was *Mr.* Nancy… Look it up, google it!"
—actor/coach **Charles Nelson Reilly**

"They used to say 'Only in America.' Well, Americans used to say it. Mostly it referred to becoming extremely rich in America. Not to social-pioneering firsts. When it comes to advances concerning women and minorities, it has seldom been in the forefront of fairness and equality—and still isn't."—heterosexual actor-activist **Corin Redgrave**, son of gay actor Sir Michael Redgrave

"American men are even more paranoid about possible tenderness between males than European men… Monty Clift ad-libbed a line in *The Search*, addressing a boy—a child, mind you—as 'dear.' He then insisted that we reshoot the scene. He was terrified of the audience's possible interpretation of that innocent word."—director **Fred Zinnemann**

"There is a superstar actor who seems to live in terror that something about his earliest days in Hollywood may become widely known: that he was employed by a top male-escort service that serviced men."—director **Gene Saks** (*Mame*), ex-husband of Bea Arthur

"When we point out that someone the mainstream public admires was gay, they accuse us of lying and wanting everyone to be gay. Like they should talk! They try and pretend everyone was straight except for a few flaming queens... As gay people we have to admit that a number of gays have been total duds... J. Edgar Hoover, to name one. A right-winger's right-winger... his biggest fear concerning Hollywood was that Rock Hudson might someday portray an FBI agent on screen."—columnist **Gay Boy Ric**

"I told a movie-buff neighbor Katharine Hepburn was gay, and she was like, 'You shouldn't say that, she's not here to defend herself.' Come again? Defend herself against what? Being different? Being who she really was? And if she was here, she'd still be in her golly-I-miss-Spencer [Tracy] closet, denying away."
—Bay Area casting director **Ann Brebner**

"Just 'cause someone died of AIDS doesn't make them some wonderful martyr. A lot of horrid people have died of AIDS, from Roy Cohn on up."—former porn star **Jack Wrangler** (Cohn, who was gay and Jewish, actively worked against the gay and Jewish communities and was a henchman to witch-hunting Republican Senator Joseph McCarthy)

"Many comedians are far from funny off-stage, and some get bitter or paranoid with age. This applies to straights, lesbians, gays, you name it... I was flabbergasted to hear Kaye Ballard call the attempt to get her to admit her personal truth 'terrorism' and Whoopi Goldberg call outing 'McCarthyism.' Just what are those gals so afraid of?"—comedian **Bob Smith**

"In Hollywood women lose marketability and income when their sex appeal fades. Young, they can be sexually ambiguous. When they're older and want to remain leading ladies they require some opposite-sex credentials. That's what started Kate Hepburn off with Spencer Tracy. But it still goes on."
—female publicist **Ronnie Chasen**

"A lesbian magazine reviewed *Hollywood Lesbians*, my book of interviews with lesbian and bi celebrities. I was surprised when the reviewer said my factually naming the women as lesbian, etc., was akin to witch-hunting... 'naming names,' she charged. Whether she was mad that she didn't do such a book first or whether she felt it's shameful to be or be called lesbian, bisexual or gay, I don't know.

"But one can't under-estimate the amount of self-hate, not to mention jealousy, that some non-heterosexuals harbor." —author-interviewer **Boze Hadleigh** (in 2016 the book was expanded and reissued as *Hollywood Lesbians: From Garbo to Foster*)

"What's handy for closeted lesbians is the cultural privilege of women being allowed more touching and affection towards each other. And if you're both attractive the culture tends or prefers to think you're not lesbians. You almost have to convince them."—openly gay **Megan Fox** (*Transformers*)

"If you're out and you go out with your boyfriend or husband, don't bring along a female friend or relative unless you don't mind the media or tabloids taking a picture and saying there you are with your girlfriend—and probably cropping your fella out of the photo!"—singer-actor **Lance Bass**

"There comes a time to stop being afraid of labels. There are always going to be labels anyway. Rise above the label-givers and make your particular label classier by being a good example of it."
—**Luke Evans** (*Dracula Untold*)

"Becoming a 'star' mostly has to do with luck… being in a big hit, in several hits. Is it worth straitjacketing yourself emotionally and sexually to gamble on that tiny chance? At any given time there's a few hundred actors who have star quality—two or three will reach stardom. Over the long run, and the short run, you're happier if you don't live inside a closet."
—**Matt Bomer**, married to publicist Simon Halls

"Clifton Webb was a movie star despite not being the 'type.' Closeted, even in private. When I'd ask about his private life or who he was seeing, all he would talk about was his mother Maybelle. They were life-long roomies."—friend and costar **Vincent Price**

"It must be tough to be orphaned at 71."
—**Noel Coward** to his pal in deep mourning Clifton Webb (*Laura, Mr. Belvedere*)

"Edward Everett Horton was super famous as a funny character actor for several decades. Gay, single, necessarily closeted for his work… super cheap [although he] owned several blocks of what became downtown Encino. To save money he moved in with his mother after she was 60. He explained in the newspaper, 'My mother took care of me when I was very young, I will now take care of her in her remaining years.'

"Well, the woman lived to over 100."
—**Bob Carroll Jr.**, who wrote 180 episodes of *I Love Lucy*

"Until society gets younger and more sophisticated I can understand a star being closeted. Comedians do not need to, most supporting performers don't, non-actor singers don't, directors don't need to…"—publicist turned novelist **Richard Condon** (*Prizzi's Honor*)

"There's a German director who was openly gay or bi back home, then he moves to Hollywood, takes up action movies and goes into the closet. He even had a gay periodical retract describing him as gay. That's what is called going Hollywood."—openly gay UK actor and novelist **Stephen Fry**

"The excuse for having only male directors and only straight male directors was that a director is a father figure. He's the boss on a set and he needs the

cast and crew's respect. Uh-huh. Directors from Dorothy Arzner and Ida Lupino on to Barbra [Streisand] and Jodie [Foster] and myself have proven otherwise. The men just want it to be a boys' club. Tough titty, guys. Your monopoly's over."
—**Penny Marshall**, the first female director to helm two films that each grossed over $100 million

"I asked Mike about what he liked to do in his spare time, nudge-nudge, and he'd tell me about books he'd read. What else besides reading? I asked. Then he listed some hobbies he wished he had time for."
—**Robin Williams** on his *Birdcage* director Mike Nichols

"All too often the truth is exiled until death supervenes. As with director Mike Nichols and celebrity photographer Richard Avedon."—reviewer **Brian Handler** on *Avedon: Something Personal*, a book revealing the two men's decade-long affair

"Comes word that a movie is being prepped about comedian turned major director Mike Nichols… it includes the cooperation of his widow Diane Sawyer. One therefore wonders if it will include any mention of his real sexuality."—columnist **Carolina Venice**

"I just can't do it. *You* do it, after I'm gone."
—**Richard Avedon** to his friend and longtime studio director Norma Stevens, about letting it be known he was gay (Avedon and Mike Nichols had planned to leave their wives and elope)

"Richard Avedon didn't come out because he didn't want to be known as a 'gay photographer.' Same reason many others in the arts don't come out... and while it's true that Picasso wasn't known as a 'straight painter,' his heterosexuality and promiscuity, his mistresses and illegitimate children, were well known and didn't affect how his art was judged.

"Saying 'I don't want to be known as a gay such-and-such' is just a cop-out, another selfish excuse."
—author **Christopher Hitchens**

"I didn't realize I was that funny. I wasn't trying to be. But that cast me as a comedian, irrevocably. It also cast me as odd... you know what I mean? I was afraid to come out for the longest time. Eventually it became too obvious to deny."—**Charles Nelson Reilly**

"Some people already dislike me. Why give them more ammunition?"—English actor **Denholm Elliott**, whose widow outed him in a book

"I like being liked. This is a homophobic society. I'd prefer not to be a homosexual... long ago I went to a psychiatrist because I was afraid I was one. He set me straight."—director **Blake Edwards** (*Breakfast at Tiffany's, Victor/Victoria*)

"I got immense flak for saying Blake Edwards was gay. I don't know about [wife] Julie Andrews. I was only stating what I thought the interviewer already knew. After that, my job was in jeopardy..."
—**Max Bercutt**, head of Warner Bros. publicity for 15 years

"I had a small part in the movie *Operation Petticoat*... Whereas [costar] Cary Grant flirted with me, its director, Blake Edwards, actually came on to me. Out of fear of his power, I declined his offer... He did tell me to stay deep in the closet, advice I'd already had drummed into me.

"After I at last did come out, virtually post-Hollywood, I could walk around in public breathing freely and not having to look to my right, to my left and behind me... How do you spell relief? O-u-t!"
—**Dick Sargent** (*Bewitched*)

"When you're in the closet you give away so many good and vital things. One thing you do keep is the fear of being ruined or blackmailed by almost anybody who finds out."—**Brandon Flynn** (*13 Reasons Why*)

"For decades people wondered if Colonel Tom Parker, Elvis Presley's manager, 'had something' on Elvis... the way he dominated him and took 50 percent of his income. Some people remarked that Elvis didn't get married for a very long time... The irony was that the so-called Colonel, who called Elvis 'my boy,' had several secrets Elvis never knew about... He was an illegal alien from Holland named Andreas Cornelis van Kuijk, he possibly killed a woman before fleeing his country forever, he made side deals for himself Elvis was unaware of, he badly mismanaged Elvis's career, he didn't let him perform overseas because he, the Colonel, couldn't leave or re-enter the USA with no passport or U.S. citizenship.

"And though Parker did marry but had no kids, several insiders noted his attachments to younger, slimmer men and his dislike of women touching him. Some said outright he was 'asexual.' But very, very few men are actually asexual..."—EP biographer **Albert Goldman**

"Colonel Parker had a longtime wife slightly older than himself who'd already divorced and had a son. No record exists anywhere that they ever married—that may have been to prevent future claims on his property if they split up... Three years after Marie died—and they were not buried together, as she and everyone had assumed—he married a female assistant. The man was old, fat and ailing and needed looking after. Plus after they got married he didn't have to pay her."—**Rick Kenyon**, a plasterer who did work for Tom Parker in Madison, TN, where Parker maintained an office

"I don't much criticize straight women, but blind? My sister was a successful legal secretary. Then she wed a showbiz lawyer, worked part-time for him— didn't get paid for it. How tough is it to see the roots of heterosexual marriage as a man acquiring property, branding it and the resultant children with his name only, and getting the woman's in-house work and services, including sexual services, for free?

"My sister once told me she was sorry I was lesbian, which temporarily ended our relationship. Years later I wasn't glad to tell her I was sorry she'd married that shmuck— left her for a starlet—and had given up her career, if not her work."—**"Josh,"** a SAG-AFTRA employee

"I worked with both Alice Ghostley and Paul Lynde… for too long, she has been called a female Paul Lynde. But I saw him copy her twitchy mannerisms and adopt them as his own. So if anything, he is the male Alice Ghostley.

"Paul wasn't a nice man. Not because he was gay… he was a mean drunk and very anti-Semitic. He believed 'the Jews' kept him from becoming a star. LOL!"—concentration camp survivor and actor **Robert Clary** (*Hogan's Heroes*)

On being referred to as the male Heidi Fleiss: "She was a madam for what, a couple of years? I did it for 15. No one, gay or straight, was more successful than I was with Brad's Buddies [Forest's company]. If anything, Heidi Fleiss is the female David Forest." **—David Forest**

"David Forest was offered a job by David Geffen booking leading musical acts. In the 1980s he struck gold hiring out porn stars to big names in Hollywood, closeted men who could afford to pay $5,000 for an hour with an 'escort.' David has files and tapes on virtually every big name on both sides of the camera, a blackmailer's Aladdin's cave… In the late '90s Forest was convicted for pandering and spent a year and a half in jail. He's gone now, but those secrets aren't dead."—**Brad X**

"The rumor is, Brad Davis hustled for a living before getting hired as an actor. He had the looks and build… and went both ways. It's not unusual, if you can't get a job and pay your rent… After he was HIV-positive Brad paid into a number of health-insurance plans but then went and paid into another one, somehow not under his own name, because he was so afraid of not getting hired if his health situation became known. A tragedy."—**Zelda Rubinstein** (*Picket Fences*)

"Some performers live in the closet due to baseless shame. Others are fine within themselves but don't want to lose career opportunities. Like Lily Tomlin, who wasn't a leading lady, let alone a sex symbol... and came out way later than most."
—Flemish-Canadian comedian **Yvette Tveidt**

"The producers of a documentary on gay characters in movies approached an openly gay novelist to write the narration. He asked 'what celebrity was going to read it?' Lily Tomlin. He said he wasn't about to write for a 'closeted dyke'—his words. The producers said it was okay because the narration would include Lily's coming-out speech. The writer signed on. She signed on. Then Tomlin cut the speech."—female film producer **J.D. Disalvatore**

"Yes, I agree a very large percentage of comediennes are lesbian... Most? I don't know about that... But give the ladies time. Most are still in the closet."—**Bea Arthur**

"There's a successful youngish-to-mid-aged female-standup comic, very androgynous even with shoulder-length hair. Absolutely lesbian but tries to hide it behind her adopted children. Wears neckties.

May or may not be celibate or asexual. Regardless, her sexual and affectional orientation is lesbian. What is she so ashamed of? "—comedian **Bill Dana**

"Okay. Comedienne Kaye Ballard is well into her 80's, has never come out. Maybe at that age we shouldn't expect it... yet once a performer's parents are dead and after they've retired, why the everlasting silence? What's a gal's excuse? Guilt over not having been poked by a man and reproduced a mini-he? There is no good excuse!"—stuntwoman **Paula Dell** (*Charlie's Angels*)

"I don't know why Earl Holliman didn't become a movie star... he had roles in lots of movies but is best known for *Police Woman* on TV. I've often seen him around town with his boyfriend. He never married [a woman] but I don't think he's ever come out."
—theatre actor **David Cravatt**

"I'll give sort of a pass to those let's face it brave actors of yore who didn't cave and marry and use a woman as a shield. Very few stars didn't give in... Some single actors eventually came out, like Richard Chamberlain and Tab Hunter. Others didn't, like Cesar Romero and, for heaven's sake, Roddy McDowall and Liberace!"—reviewer **Brian Handler**

"It's great when sexy, popular actors flirt in interviews with the notion of bisexuality. In one of those Barbara Walters interviews, Burt Reynolds named some handsome actors he said were so attractive he 'could be bisexual for them.' That took guts! Even if he later married and divorced Loni Anderson.

"Then, during *Desperate Housewives* James Denton did a *TV Guide* interview where he said maybe his character should have a same-sex affair. I think Denton's straight, I know Burt's bi, but either way, thanks, guys!"—actor **Alexis Arquette** (brother of Rosanna and Patricia)

"We were in this little town on the edge of the Sahara, and there was nothing to do at night except go to this disco. But it was all men dancing with men because women weren't allowed out at night. So we're standing at the bar, watching all these guys dancing, when Sean [Connery] leans over and says to me, 'Do you mind if I dance with your driver? Mine's too ugly.'"—**Michael Caine**, on the shooting of *The Man Who Would Be King*

"Hollywood presumes if the audience is uncomfortable they'll stay out of the theatres. Or I guess tell their friends to. So when it's a gay-themed picture, especially if there's a love scene, they cast straight actors so the audience can think, they're not actually *enjoying* that kiss, they're only acting it. Like with Christopher Reeve and Michael Caine [in *Deathtrap*]. Ahem, but Caine is straight… and… I won't say any more."—actress **Doris Roberts**, whose second husband was bisexual

"I always had a fantasy that Superman was bisexual. Because he's so powerful and above-human that he couldn't be limited to silly human prejudices. I got more of a Superman crush when I found out he was created by two young Jewish guys and the big S on his chest is the first letter of each of their last names."—gay historian **Martin Greif**

"Comic-book super-heroes are often semi closeted. With their secret identities... like working stiff Clark Kent who secretly flies all over the world and displays his buff bod in tights... Or Batman's alter ego Bruce Wayne and his boyish ward Dick Grayson. The real personality hides behind a more normative façade."—psychotherapist Dr. **Betty Berzon**

"The network suits were very nervous about having no romantic implications between Batman and Robin the wonderful boy—did I say that? I meant Robin the Boy Wonder. But myriad viewers still caught some kind of lavender vibe. Hey, we were both great-looking. I still look good, anyway."
—Batman/Bruce Wayne **Adam West**

"On the original *Star Trek* William Shatner didn't get along with George Takei, who he knew was gay. Decades later when George came out and became this online and media gay icon, it irked Shatner. Leonard [Nimoy] used to say Bill could never get enough publicity. He only wanted to share a portion of it with Len."—**Bill Lutz**, 1960s TV casting director

"First you had a Jewish Mr. Spock. Leonard Nimoy based his Vulcan greeting on Jewish symbolism. Shatner seldom refers to his own Jewishness... Now you have a gay Mr. Spock, via [openly gay] Zachary Quinto. That's great, why not? Nature, including human nature, is about variety."—straight actor **Louis Zorich** (*Mad About You*)

"You could have knocked me over with a feather when I heard openly gay George Takei—hey, it rhymes—was disappointed that Sulu, the character George first played, is a gay character in the latest *Star Trek* movie. Where is his logic? I doubt it stems from self-hate. But anything's possible. Actors and their egos…"—**Bonnie Tiegel**, senior producer of TV's *Entertainment Tonight*

"I was desperate to be outed, but nobody would publish the fact. Lots of journalists believe they're protecting you by not putting it into their articles."
—actor turned playwright (*The Stand-In*) **Keith Curran**

"No, no, no. Closeted stars are very well protected. Even the semi-closeted ones. You almost have to force a magazine or newspaper, at gun-point, to intimate, much less state, that somebody is gay, lesbian or bi."—columnist **Lance Browne** of The Hollywood Kids

"When he got himself arrested for brawling in a gay bar, he outed himself. Case closed."—*New York Post* columnist **Richard Johnson**, reporting on 10/4/98 about James Caan's son Scott Caan (*Hawaii Five-O*), who with a male companion allegedly assaulted two other males at a West Hollywood gay bar
In contrast, the *Chicago Tribune* gave no gender to Caan's "date," while Reuters News Service— reportedly then owned by virulently anti-gay televangelist Pat Robertson—went so far as to claim the jealousy-inspired fight was "over a woman."

"I tell screenwriters, don't use 'gay,' it doesn't mean what it used to. And don't use that word to mean what it now means, because then it just promotes homosexuality."—movie director **George Sidney** (*Kiss Me Kate, Show Boat*), seemingly unaware that some 99% of the media promotes heterosexuality

"This is a dangerous subject."—TV talk host **Tom Snyder** on the phone to this writer before eventually booking me in 1993 to discuss *The Lavender Screen*, about LGBT+-themed films, most of them starring heterosexuals

"Tom Snyder had strange ideas about boys 'being turned' gay. During a 1993 station break our off-air topic was early sexual experiences. I told Tom I saw my first erection in the Vatican. His jaw dropped. I explained it was on a classical statue, not a priest. In those days you could be alone in many rooms of the huge Vatican Museum, where I'd wandered off from my professor father, mother and sister.

"At age 12, in that pre-'information highway' age, I was dumbfounded as to *why* the handsome statue's thing was like *that*. Later, I was surprised the statue had been on public view—erections and art depicting gay sex are invariably hidden in museum storerooms. Sixteen years after, when I returned to Rome, the Vatican Museum was disappointingly crowded—no way could you be alone in any room—and of course that statue was nowhere to be seen."—author **Boze Hadleigh**

"I never say in interviews, when I do them, that I am [heterosexual]. But when I enacted a gay man living under Italy's fascist regime I was asked to confirm it. I did not. I am an actor. I play dozens of men. Do I have to explain that?"—**Marcello Mastroianni**, Oscar-nominated for *Una Giornata Particolare* (*A Special Day*)

"We have northern blond Italians with blue eyes. Hollywood shows only the southern Italian brown eyes and olive skin... There are obvious and non-obvious homosexuals—but Hollywood shows the kind that right away you know. It is all stereotyping but also it is laziness."—heterosexual **Ugo Tognazzi** of the Franco-Italian gay comedy *La Cage Aux Folles*

"James Caan, who has an allegedly gay actor son, isn't ranked as a significant talent. But he did a French film, Le*s Uns et Les Autres* [1982, *The Ones and the Others*], playing a man and his gay son. He went the less obvious route by playing the adult son as a man who happens to be gay... rather than the stereotype that got William Hurt an American Oscar for *Kiss of the Spider Woman*... Hollywood prefers the flashy and the overdone... and no one there's ever heard of that French film."—UK playwright **Pam Gems** (*Piaf*)

"I played a homosexual in the stage musical *La Cage Aux Folles*. If you do it more than once people may get the wrong idea."
—straight Jewish actor **Gene Barry**, born Eugene Klass

"Yeah, I've played gay... and for a while that and what somebody called my 'angelic face' had some people convinced I was gay. No worries. This is a chameleon-like business."—**Paul Rudd**

"Rock [Hudson] was considered handsome rather than talented. He wasn't a bad actor at all—in some five dozen movies he convincingly played straight men. Only straight men, to keep audiences from getting the right idea."—**Drew Barrymore**

"Hollywood preferred to closet everyone. If you were Jewish you changed your name and said Merry Christmas. If you were Latino you changed your name and tried to get rid of your accent. If you were gay you married a woman. If… and on and on."
—Jewish star **Paul Newman**

"You have celebrities like Whitney Houston who resist coming out as gay or bi because already they're one minority and don't want to be two minorities. In her case she also has a very religious mother who believes lesbians can't fall in love."—novelist **Jackie Collins**

"Some people are more brave, less selfish. Look at Johnny Mathis, who came out in the 1980s and continued his career. It helped that he was a singer, not an actor who had to do opposite-sex love scenes. But still brave of him, during the Reagan era."
—**Elizabeth Montgomery** (*Bewitched*)

"It's not unusual for famous people to engage in 'marriages of convenience.' It is unusual for the son of someone famous. But if the office, political office, is big enough… I refer to Ron Reagan Jr., who says he's pro-gay. That's *all* he says…"—columnist **Boyd McDonald**

"'Marriage of convenience' is a misnomer if you don't have money and are stuck together all the time.

But the VIPs who undertake such marriages, whether either or both partners are non-heterosexual, often live apart, without the public being any the wiser."
—romance novelist **Barbara Cartland**

"John [Travolta] is overly concerned with what people think of him. He's no longer Tony Manero (in *Saturday Night Fever*) or Danny Zuko (in *Grease*). That was the 1970s… He hasn't come out into the 21st century."—**Carrie Fisher**

"I think it's important that George Michael got caught with his trousers down. I've been telling him to come out for ten years. There's no excuse in this day and age, especially for somebody with $50 million in the bank, to be in the closet."—**Boy George**

"There was no one else in that Beverly Hills restroom with George Michael except the policeman who had nothing better to do than try and entrap the guy, so what's the crime, so-called? Shouldn't such entrapment be a crime by now?"—UK singer **Jimmy Somerville**, who was denied entry into the U.S. after he was similarly entrapped in London

"Public figures are role models and have responsibilities. GLBTQ youth need role models. The rate of gay teen suicide is obscenely higher than for straight teens. Nobody should kill themselves out of shame and because gay stars are too cowardly or greedy to come out of the closet!"—**George Michael**, after coming out

"There's so damn few positive black gay role models. Most whites think there are almost no gay blacks except for drag queens like RuPaul. All these closeted actors like Paul Winfield and Sherman Hemsley of *The Jeffersons*, not to mention all the ones on the down-low. It's a crime they don't at some point come out, 'cause young gay black males are the most vulnerable of all."—writer **E. Lynn Harris**

"[Michael Jackson] threw a temper tantrum when Lisa Marie's two-year-old son pulled off his wig. [Although] she admonished him, Michael stormed out and took a jet to Paris with two young boys whom he has taken on trips before. The boys stayed in the hotel room with Jackson and accompanied him to Euro Disneyland."—*Spy* magazine in 1996

"The air-conditioning remained on throughout the interview, causing an unusual noise in the background… It couldn't be shut off because the lights on [Michael] Jackson were so hot that his thick pancake makeup and lipstick would have melted and his false eyelashes would have come off."
—anonymous **soundman** at the taping of Diane Sawyer's interview of Jackson and Lisa Marie Presley

"We need a campaign to shame the media into being honest about gay people, including gay celebrities and role models—sports figures too, even though they're seldom role models any more. We need to state and reiterate how many gay and lesbian teens kill themselves all because of homophobia. That has got to stop!"—**Christopher Isherwood**

"The Establishment and its mainstream press is anti-outing. Yet outing is merely telling the truth. Nobody 'outs' heterosexuals. And it no longer ruins careers."
—playwright **Edward Albee** (*Three Tall Women)*

"Even after Jodie Foster finally came out, the mass media wouldn't provide the information that her real name was Alicia. Her mother's live-in girlfriend Josephine Dominguez was nicknamed Jo D., so the girl became Jodie... The mass media would rather ignore the whole topic."—talk show host **John Cluckie**

"I'm not sure why... maybe some of my roles or being a feminist, but in the past some people have thought I was a lesbian. I don't care. That's a nice thing to be... Love is so rare that no one should ever try to stifle it. We should encourage all love relationships to blossom... It's all beautiful, and it's all so rare."
—**Liv Ullmann**

"Saying somebody was lesbian or gay hurt individuals only because society as a whole agreed to enforce homophobia and punish people for not being heterosexual. In the 1950s it hurt a glamorous movie star named Lizabeth Scott. A mean-spirited magazine named *Confidential* outed her. Ms. Scott was even criticized for being Jewish... her real name was Emma Matzo."
—Jewish actress **Doris Roberts** (*Everybody Loves Raymond*)

"Angela Lansbury finally did admit her first husband was gay, and that's why she wouldn't marry another actor. She hadn't known, and understandably felt betrayed... Doris Roberts I don't think has

80

admitted her second husband, a writer, was bisexual—dunno if she knew when she married him."
—actress **Joyce Van Patten**

"Hollywood's top hairdresser, in the closet. Sydney Guilaroff published a memoir. Its launch party brought several female celebs out, so to speak... Angela Lansbury, who had a gay husband... a certain First Lady who had a gay son... In the book Mr. Guilaroff came out. As Jewish. An amazing surprise!

"And pretended he'd had affairs with Garbo and Ava Gardner and that his lovers were his adopted sons and grandsons. Talk about chutzpah."
—composer **Hugh Martin** ("The Trolley Song" from *Meet Me in St. Louis*)

"I wrote my book because when I grew up there was no such book, and if mine could help just one kid out there who's secretly gay then it's worth it."
—Broadway icon **Tommy Tune**, whose memoir served as his coming-out

"It's important for young people—no, all people—to know our unofficial national anthem 'America the Beautiful' comes down to us from a lesbian professor, Katharine Lee Bates. She wrote it after experiencing a scenic cross-country train trip... Bates had a 30-year marriage to a fellow Wellesley instructress.

"Remember her name. Katharine is spelled as in Hepburn, then Lee like Harper Lee who wrote *To Kill a Mockingbird,* but no relation to closet-y Anthony Perkins or his alter ego Norman Bates."
—*Out* magazine cofounder **Sarah Petit**

"Greedy relatives… if a late star has a straight image he's more marketable to his heirs when they write a book about him… or more profitable via movie or TV residuals. I notice one of Cary Grant's ex-wives, a former star, wrote a book about him. So did the daughter, who deplores anybody thinking daddy wasn't straight. 'Where is the love?' she asks. Well, where is the reality? The tolerance? The acceptance of people who are gay or bisexual? Grow up, kid!"
—comedian **Garry Shandling**

"Most actors think they have a book in them, and perhaps they do. And there it should usually remain. Because actors act on paper too."—two-time Oscar winner turned Member of Parliament turned actor **Glenda Jackson**

"My husband was also the father of my two sons… After all those years, when he decided to tell me he was what he called bisexual, I had to doubt myself as a woman. I felt so unattractive. I just kept wondering… about so many things."—**Charlotte Rae** (*Diff'rent Strokes, The Facts of Life*)

"You can't print this, but I think his battering me was frustration over his being, say, AC/DC. Burt was definitely drawn to men. His father was a police chief… his desires were a real conflict for Burt. So for a time he took it out on me. I left him after he banged my head against the wall."
—British actress **Judy Carne** (*Rowan & Martin's Laugh-In*), first wife of Burt Reynolds

"It's been revealed that Cary Grant beat his first wife, an actress who worked with Charlie Chaplin but gave up acting after marriage. Grant was very angry at having to marry, he was very involved with Randolph Scott, the real love of his life before, during and some say after all the wives. In later years Grant made fun of marriage."—Oscar-winning actress **Claire Trevor**, a close friend of Rock Hudson

"The fundamentalists want every gay man to marry a woman. How happy a marriage, and how fair to the woman, do they think that would be? Of course they usually don't give a damn about women's happiness, nor fairness in general. There's anything but fun in fundamentalism."
—comedian **Scott Thompson**

"Elizabeth Taylor's first husband, the [heterosexual] son of Conrad Hilton, beat her up. Including when she was pregnant. For husband number two she turned to an older, gentle, bisexual English actor, Michael Wilding, later declaring that they ended up like brother and sister. But because Wilding fathered her two sons she never conceded that he went both ways."
—Taylor biographer **C. David Heymann**

"Elizabeth Taylor encourages actors to come out of the closet. But when her pal Michael Jackson's own doctor admitted Jackson was gay, Elizabeth was furious. When the press outed her pretend-boyfriend Malcolm Forbes, she was furious. Seems it's easier to be pro-gay about strangers and dead costars."
—Hollywood costume designer **Ray Aghayan**

"Why were Elizabeth Taylor and Michael Jackson such close friends? They were really much closer in public... Michael consistently showered Liz with expensive gifts, partly to retain her friendship. She gave him respectability, which he sorely needed with all the pedophilia charges, and he gave Liz, in the twilight of her career, publicity and made her seem hip."
—**Joe Hyams**, publicist (45 years at Warner Bros.)

"Richard Jenkins changed his name to Richard Burton after the gay schoolmaster he idolized and moved in with. When he became famous his official bio said he moved in with Burton as a small boy. But it was well into Richard's teens... Richard stayed in touch with Burton all his life and included him in his will. Burton outlived Richard."—**Roddy McDowall**, who costarred with Richard Burton on Broadway in *Camelot*

"I read a quote by Richard Burton... he believed most actors are secretly or latently homosexual and 'cover it with drink.' An exaggeration, but he'd have lived much longer had he not been a chronic alcoholic."—UK actress **Joan Hickson**, aka Agatha Christie's Miss Marple

"I know English actors who are out in London and in the closet in Los Angeles... This makes me angry because it sends a terrible message and is selfish and unkind and it underestimates the audience."
—Sir **Ian McKellen**

"Some people misunderstand being out. They think it means no privacy and every private detail

becoming known. Not at all. Stating the simple fact that you're gay doesn't mean saying who you're sleeping with or how you're sleeping with them."
—**Chad Allen** (*Dr. Quinn, Medicine Woman*)

"It [being gay] is in ways comparable to being left-handed, a minority that in olden days was often vilified. 'Left' in French is *gauche*, in Latin it's *sinister*. Machines are designed for the right-handed majority… every year hundreds of industrial accidents occur because of that. And there's no country or culture where left-handeds are the majority. Am I left-handed? I'll never tell! Ha-ha."—**Lady Gaga**

"If you say you're gay or lesbian I don't ask for details. If you say you're left-handed I don't ask what you do with your left hand when alone."
—**Benedict Cumberbatch** (*The Imitation Game*)

"Your sexuality is such a part of your creativity, and acting is a creative and emotional profession. Your sexuality conditions your emotions and responses and interactions. A talented actor cannot be emotionally constipated."—**Randy Harrison** (*Queer as Folk*)

"Closets stand for prisons, not privacy."
—lesbian comedian **Robin Tyler**

"The tabloids sent reporters to visit the women's neighbors, posing as a gay-rights group. Tired of the spying and the bigoted reportage, Amanda chose to finally come out publicly." —from this writer's ***Hollywood Lesbians: From Garbo to Foster***, about *Married with*

Children actor-turned-director Amanda Bearse and her female partner and their adopted baby daughter

"If someone is chasing you, stop running. And then they'll stop chasing you."—**Cynthia Nixon** in *New York* magazine; the openly bi *Sex in the City* actress later ran for New York governor

"Being in the closet is a lot harder than being out… you don't *know* that when you're in… I came out by kissing Geraldo Rivera during his show. I'd been performing for ten years… people have since been very supportive, very giving. And I've doubled my income since then too."—comedian **Jason Stuart**

"No one wants to be categorized as just one thing. But when it comes to sexuality, you either label yourself or they do it for you. After all, you are basically one or the other, so 'fess up!"—British rock star **Marc Bolan**

"I think David Bowie is the only example of somebody who came out and later went back in." —singer **Michael Hutchence**, INXS

"Anne Heche was becoming a movie star. She and Ellen DeGeneres were the most publicized lesbian couple since Gertrude Stein and Alice B. Toklas. Everyone saw that photo of them next to President Clinton… Then one day Anne left—no one but Ellen knows what really happened… Anne wrote a book titled *Call Me Crazy* that I read and which explained nothing."—actress **Delores Taylor** (*Billy Jack*)

"We writers always know who's gay, and we don't point it out... The general public don't mind knowing that Mike Tyson beats his wife. That's something they can identify with. They can't identify with lesbians—it's too scary."
—columnist **Janet Charlton** in 1990

"Of course little is said or printed about stars who shone before vaudeville, radio, movies, television, video, etc., etc. But America's very first star, by general consensus, was a lesbian named Charlotte Cushman. She should be a household name."
—publicist **Andrea Jaffe**

"History's first major female ruler may well have been lesbian... The pharaoh Hatshepsut took over the throne of Egypt from her late husband's young son and depicted herself in paintings and statues as a male ruler, complete with symbolic beard."
—historian **Barbara Tuchman**

"I visited Portugal after the death of the long-running fascist dictator Salazar, who never married. In Lisbon I asked a cab driver—who admitted she was gay—whether Salazar had been secretly gay. She was near-scandalized by the idea. Oh, no, she insisted, he'd had a maid who was his mistress... I'd expect that type of desperate closeting from a straight man, even a straight woman, but from a lesbian? A lesbian Lisbon cab driver? It's like the fascism still survived."
—travel guide and writer **Edwina Gibson**

"Having an official girlfriend is part of the closeting game, be it England or Hollywood. I remember Boy

George saying the romance between George Michael and his supposed girlfriend was as probable as Boy George romancing a door. And by now [2019] most everyone's heard about the Scientology star who was assigned a girlfriend after the head Scientologist's wife auditioned actresses for the role! The news came out from a top Scientology executive who defected, who'd been there witnessing those auditions."—**Colin**, a UK actor and former Scientologist

"To join a homophobic cult if you're gay you have to be ruthlessly ambitious or brimming with self-hate. Or both. Unfortunately Hollywood abounds with many such warped personalities."—**Tim Flack**, CBS VP of Creative Affairs

"I was introduced to [New York City mayor Ed] Koch at a party in 1982, specifically to talk about AIDS. And the minute he knew what I wanted to talk about I was hauled away by police. He was a closeted gay man and did not want in any way to be associated with that."—writer and activist **Larry Kramer** in 1998

"Outing began as a counter-measure against publicly homophobic politicians and preachers, etc., who were privately homosexual. Their harmful and hypocritical homophobia had to be exposed."
—bisexual poet **Rod McKuen**

"Once in a blue moon closeting can help, very rarely. A single man got elected governor of a certain state back when people never imagined anyone was gay unless he was a caricature. Later, with more public awareness of gay men, that man had to marry a woman to get elected governor again. The gay community didn't out him because he is pro-gay, he's equal rights for everybody. If you have to lie to do good, so be it."—anonymous **California political analyst**

"Truman Capote was positively gleeful when he was able to out Cardinal Spellman, a very influential, deeply closeted churchman and very vocal public homophobe. Truman had to wait till Spellman died. That's what's changed. Now you out the hypocrites while they're alive and hopefully prevent them doing more damage."—actor/coach **Charles Nelson Reilly**

"To me, it's harmful when longtime same-sex couples deny being gay. As if gay relationships mean nothing, no matter how long. Like Siegfried and Roy. I mean, they're Las Vegas, not Hollywood. Who doesn't know they're gay? Shirley MacLaine outed them years ago. But mum's the word."
—singer **Lesley Gore** ("It's My Party")

"Sometimes being outed by someone else is a first step toward coming out yourself... Suzanne Somers attended Barry Manilow's wedding [to another man] and outed him. Then finally he came out. Taking that first step is pretty daunting."
—publicist **Paul Bloch**

"Outing usually isn't meant in a mean way, and of course heterosexuals aren't outed as gay—what would be the point? But some performers try and out their competitors, gay or not, as Frank Sinatra did with [gay singer] Johnnie Ray and then Elvis Presley, who wasn't gay, in fact didn't like gays."—music critic **Pietro Cavaluzzi**

"Somebody once called me a sissy because I'm polite… There's a 'man' in 'manners.'" —**Elvis Presley**, whom the far-right John Birch Society originally described as "a perverting, communistically-inspired menace to the sound morals of American youth"

"Two guys live together, everyone assumes they're *doing* it… Two women live together, like live together 40 years, and everyone figures it's a 'Boston [sexless] marriage.' At least that's how people *used* to think… nowadays they might suspect you if you live alone with your dog."—comedian **Phyllis Diller**

"Whatever the nature of William and Anne Shakespeare's relationship, it is worth noting that in all his canon of works there is not one depiction of a happy marriage."—historian **Erik Milford**

"This famous actor travels with his wife and his male lover, and the kids stay at home. The lover, seemingly an employee, blends into the background, while everyone comments on the husband and wife's togetherness. Of course they're always together—the husband is paranoid and takes her everywhere so the public doesn't get the right idea."—*Hollywood Studio* magazine columnist **Lee Graham**

"Liz Smith feels justified in reporting fake marriages as real ones… because it's not easy to know

if nothing goes on behind closed doors and because otherwise, she says, she'd 'have to question 80 percent of the marriages' she writes about."
—screenwriter **Helen Deutsch** (*Valley of the Dolls*)

"Hollywood is the one place, or business, where the average lesbian does get married to a man."
—**Diane Murphy**, one of twins (herself openly gay and no longer acting) who played Tabitha on *Bewitched*

"Outing is usually viewed negatively. It's not negative. However, if you say somebody gay is gay and that person responds with no, I'm not, the media prefers the lie. They go with anti-gay rather than pro-gay."—Oscar winner **Emma Thompson** (*Howards End*)

"And then there's the opposite of outing: *inning*. Like Robert Wagner alleging he had an affair with older-woman costar Barbara Stanwyck in *Titanic*, whose top-billed star was gay-as-a-goose older man Clifton Webb. Oh, what a tangled web…"—former actor **Jack Larson** (Jimmy Olson on TV's *Superman*)

"I came out late in life. Better late than never… I tried to convince [composer] Aaron Copland to come out—in his eighties. He thought it was too late. It's never too late."—**Leonard Bernstein**

"I came out at 83 [as bisexual] and it's one of the smartest things I've ever done."—**Joel Grey**, Oscar winner for *Cabaret*

"Coming out of the closet is like exhaling... being in it is like constantly inhaling in public."
—actress (*Married with Children*) turned director **Amanda Bearse**

"Being in the closet hurt my career way more than being out."—**Ellen Page**

"I'd love to come out, but I'm not a lesbian. I really wish I were."—**Cassandra** "Elvira, Mistress of the Dark" **Peterson**

"I'm willing for people to think I'm gay."
—**Madonna**

"I don't care if people think I'm gay, bi, whatever."
—**Richard Gere**, prior to taking out a full-page newspaper ad that stated otherwise

"My country [Denmark] has been at the forefront of human rights, including the gay people's rights... I used to say that I dated Cary Grant. I did. As a cover-up, arranged by his studio. It's not so easy to tell the truth but yes, it was a cover-up."—**Greta Thyssen**, who doubled for Marilyn Monroe

"The moment Chevy Chase started outing Cary Grant on the air, I knew lawyers would get involved. Mr. Grant had no choice... he had to address the situation. I did realize that any lawsuit would not go to trial. Mr. Grant didn't want his private life examined."—TV talk show host **Tom Snyder** during a commercial break to Boze Hadleigh, promoting his 1993 book *The Lavender Screen*

"I wish you could sue periodicals and papers that lie and say someone lesbian or gay isn't, or that totally ignore someone's spouse, mate, life partner... Like *TV Guide* when it said Sara Gilbert from *Roseanne* was having a baby with her partner, then omitted the partner's gender. Or when they did an obit for Raymond Burr—*Perry Mason*—and left out his husband of over 30 years. They call that 'reporting'? Liars!"—**Gilbert Baker**, creator of the Rainbow Flag

"One of the threats used against young gays, to scare them, was that they'd never have someone to love if they didn't get married... and they'd wind up alone in old age—the way so many old people in rest homes are alone because their devoted children don't come to see them."—**Graham Chapman** (*The Life of Brian*)

"I was afraid as a teen that if I acknowledged that I preferred my own kind my family would stop loving me. We do tend to underestimate our families. Sadly, some kids are dead-right about their families."
—singer/composer **Peter Allen**

"I have certain relatives that if I were sure they'd cut me off if I came out, I'd go back in the closet just to come out to them!"—composer/singer **Paul Jabara**

"Stop asking permission from the straight world to be who we are. It has nothing to do with them."
—**Boy George**

"We'd have most of our civil rights today if we didn't spend far too much time and effort over what non-gays think of us and bitching with each other."
—**Robert LaTourneaux** ("Cowboy" in *The Boys in the Band*)

"I'm not one of those people who says, 'Why do we have to label?' Openly straight people have no problem being called 'straight.' The media never call someone an accomplished gay person—they think that's out of line. But they have no problem calling Andrew Cunanan 'the gay murderer.'"—columnist **Michael Musto**

"Intimidation isn't always through legal threats. A guy who had an affair with Dom DeLuise was going onto a TV talk show whose theme of the day was closeted actors. Some Italian American friends of Dom warned the guy to temporarily leave town for his health. He never did show on the talk show."
—Hollywood publicist **Paul Bloch**

"What's sad and mystifying is that the tranny [male] prostitute who got caught with Eddie Murphy and was reaching out to the media to talk about him died in a freak accident about a year later… unsolved. I'm not implying anything, but sometimes a big mouth in Hollywood is a dangerous liability."
—San Francisco casting director **Ann Brebner**

"You'd think a member of a minority would think twice before insulting another minority member in a 'comedy' routine. But some people are plain stupid or malicious."—talk show host **Carol Vitale** on Eddie Murphy

"When you tell your family you're gay, then it's not such a remote issue… maybe they'll think twice before telling a fag joke again or laughing at one."
—**Wilson Cruz** (*My So-Called Life*)

"Damon Wayans of *In Living Color* would do routines based on gay-bashing. His humor was so vicious that some gays would get up and walk out on his act, and then he'd tell the audience there were no longer any 'fags' in the room."—San Francisco comedian and almost-mayor **Tom Ammiano**

"With more time on my hands I follow the news more. I don't live in San Francisco and I'm not gay but it's time the 'gay capital' gets an openly gay mayor. My vote goes to Mark Leno. No relation to Jay; he's Jewish. I find older gay men appealing… they keep up their looks, slim and well-dressed… there's usually more charm and friendliness."—**Margot Kidder**, who played Lois Lane to Christopher Reeve's Superman (Leno lost in June 2018 by some 2,000 votes)

"It's surprising how many out celebrities didn't come out voluntarily. Either they were outed and at the time denied being gay or they were discovered in a compromising situation, like some of our Congressmen, and chose to admit it. We need more incentives for people to come out."—**Jane Lynch** (*Glee*)

"I didn't like being outed in the tabloids, but it did push me to decide to come out, which I wish I'd done long ago."—**Dick Sargent** (*Bewitched*)

"If I'd been outed in *Vanity Fair* or some classy periodical… not in a tabloid, which they're always bigoted and act like they're shaming you. Just report it the same way you'd say that it turns out somebody happens to be left-handed. Don't judge!"
—**Glenn Hughes**, "Leatherman" of the Village People

"I hated being outed. There was no dignity to it, and it made me feel powerless. But living a life in the closet is worse."—the former **Chastity**, now **Chaz**, **Bono**

"My sexual preference… is nobody's business. I would never say whether I slept with men or women. I'm just old-fashioned."
—Olympic diver **Greg Louganis** in 1988 (never say never…)

"I'll never tell. I want people to die of curiosity."
—**Queen Latifah** (ditto…)

"I was wondering if anybody noticed the irony of my receiving my Oscar from John Travolta and Queen Latifah. And you know who I saw backstage after I won? Jodie Foster. I was like, 'What is the universe telling me?' And they're all looking like, 'Congratulations, loudmouth!'"—singer/composer **Melissa Etheridge** in 2007 to syndicated gay press writer Lawrence Ferber (Queen and Jodie later came out)

"I love everybody. I think Melanie Griffith is smart. I love everybody. And John Travolta is straight as an arrow. And Jackie Chan is hung. I love everybody. April Fool's!"—**Joan Rivers** in her book *Diary of a Mad Diva*

"I doubt at my age [great-looking forties] coming out could really hurt my career... But maybe the main thing that deters me is the word 'lesbian.' I know it's mostly a lie or stereotype, but lesbians are supposed to be ugly. That's what most people think of right away when they hear the word. And so much of my image and career and my own self-image are tied to looking good. I'm sorry."—anonymous **female star**

"Showbiz is a very 'looksist' business. Gay men still want to appeal to women fans, just as lesbian actresses want to appeal to male fans. Also, actors are insecure and often want desperately to be liked. These two factors inhibit many gay performers from being open." —British actress **Judy Carne**

"For a while there I tried to be perceived as bisexual, thinking that meant everybody could like me!"—Sir **Elton John**

"I don't see why they lump us together. The transsexual is no longer a homosexual. It is a man who is attracted to men who seemingly becomes a woman and is still attracted to men, which reads as heterosexual. It is also a woman attracted to women who seemingly becomes a man and is still attracted to women, which reads as heterosexual. What is 'gay' about *that*?"—**Quentin Crisp**

"Drag queens often make convincing and beautiful females—more feminine than most real women. But the guys who actually become women... most are unconvincing-looking women. And the body switch doesn't impact the person's mind. It's still a male mind."—*Out* magazine cofounder **Sarah Petit**

"I was repulsed when former-Bruce-now-Caitlin Jenner, during the elections, kept making vicious anti-Hillary public comments and endorsing Trump. I wonder how Caitlin felt when Trump inevitably came out against transsexuals?"—Paramount executive **Linda Wohl**

"Homosexuality is not a choice. Becoming a transsexual is. I mean, if every gay man chose to become a woman, there would be no gay rights. I admire the gay man who toughs it out and lives truthfully. I don't condemn transsexuals, but I don't feel they contribute to gay rights or to women's rights."—gay actor **Taylor Negron**

"If you're hiding it, you're ashamed of it… and you're giving license to others to consider it your dirty secret."—**Russell King**, gay deputy news editor of the *New York Times*

"Straights are never ashamed to admit they're straight, and some of them should be!"
—actor (*Dobie Gillis*) turned California politician **Sheila James Kuehl**

"Some minorities can no longer be held down, [but] gays can, and because most gays are in the closet and won't speak for themselves, conservatives can keep demonizing them and can drive tremendous fundraising and votes this way.

"Don't show them as our relatives, don't show them as loving people with relationships, just show them as sex maniacs and pretend they're a huge menace—predators and civilization-destroyers—rather than the victims and culture-makers that they tend to be."—heterosexual musician **Frank Zappa**

"The more people that come out, the closer we are to equal rights."—**George Michael**

Chapter Three
Loving in Private

The lifestyles of the rich and famous have always intrigued the public, but until the last several decades their private lives were mostly guarded, by themselves and the media. Celebrity journalism has since proliferated to an undreamed-of extent, and the truth will usually out *if* one's a straight celeb. But the closeted (stars) and the closeting (media) persist, presenting the public with a false and profitable façade. In private, X may spend less time with the wife and kids than he does working and networking, socializing and sexualizing with gay pals in and out of the business, also cruising strangers in a variety of settings. Yet, in articles and on magazine covers X is "a devoted family man."

Fortunately, outside Hollywood more and more LGBT+ people realize that admitting to a gay private life isn't about revealing sex habits, it's about taking pride in one's identity and, if one has one, in one's life partner.

"Is Hugh or isn't Hugh?"—**graffito** seen on four separate sites in Sydney, referring to Australian actor Hugh Jackman

"Is She or Is She Not the Marrying Kind?"
—**1950s tabloid headline**, referring to "glamorpuss actress" Lizabeth Scott (she wasn't)

"Daddy warned me about men and alcohol. But he never said a thing about women and cocaine!"
—**Tallulah Bankhead**

"You see the handsome movie star in public. Cameras are there, so that you can see him. With his wife. Or his girlfriend. But what counts, what is *real*, is private—who you and I do *not* see him with."
—Spanish director **Pedro Almodóvar**

"Wondering how famous gay actors have sex with men who won't blackmail them? Early in a career, that's no problem… When and if stardom is achieved, stars often have sex only with other stars— or at least with actors successful enough that blackmail could work both ways."—columnist **Liz Smith**

"A very few, very expensive male escort services are reliable enough for the gay VIP. They're usually by referral only and they don't advertise. Even top politicians use these services… including one Canadian prime minister and one California governor."
—**Dack Rambo** (*Dallas*)

"Much or most Hollywood entertaining is done using caterers… there are caterers and there are caterers. Some are known to employ attractive and ambitious young actors who won't make a fuss if a gay celebrity comes on to them. Our agency is one such."

—anonymous **catering co-director**

"There's a still rather sexy but not-too-bright star who makes the tabloids for propositioning pool men, masseurs, physical trainers, caterers, etc. He also visits bathhouses in Los Angeles's Koreatown. Only in Koreatown. Maybe he figures he won't be recognized —as in, all Caucasians look alike."—**Tony Rosato** (*Saturday Night Live*)

"I was asked one time if Gilligan and the Skipper were lovers. That is the dumbest question I've ever been asked."—**Bob Denver** (*Gilligan's Island*)

"A reporter once asked me when I first knew I was gay. I said to him, 'About the same time you knew you were straight.'"—**Sir Ian McKellen**

"Do not ask a woman if her husband is bisexual. She either does not know—his 'bi' activity is away from her—or she says no because if she says yes you think he is gay... Some men truly are bisexual. Whether anyone is 50-50 bisexual is so far unknown... As long as there is bigotry people will lie.

"A brave minority will tell the truth; they are the only ones who help to improve things. Lying does not help the Situation."—French director **Agnes Varda**

"When I was up for the draft the man interviewing me asked, 'Do you like girls?' Had he been less shall we say Neanderthal I would have replied, 'Yes. I also like apple pie, but I don't want to sleep with it either.'"—early American transsexual **Christine** (born George) **Jorgensen**

102

"Is that all there is?"—**Ellen DeGeneres**, on her heterosexual experience

"The fundamentalists, besides lying without conscience, misemploy words. They keep throwing 'unnatural' at us. If they want natural, arsenic is natural. So are two-headed calves and tsunamis and cancer and Ebola, etc. What seems to be unnatural is religious obsessives keeping their fictions and bigotries to their cranky selves."
—author **Christopher Hitchens**

"The only unnatural sex is that which you cannot perform."—**Colette**

"My twin brother was gay and he was my only outlet when we moved to this country [from Jamaica]. He took me to gay bars and I loved it… people who looked much nicer and seemed to enjoy themselves more. They seemed freer. I suppose because of that I became like a gay man."—singer/actor **Grace Jones**

"The only gay stars in Turkey are drag queens and transsexuals. In a culture so extremely macho, men cannot accept a gay man who acts like a man— that would shatter their illusions and self-esteem… Drag and trans prostitutes are popular because it retains the illusion of a man having sex with or being serviced by a woman. Even the average gay Middle Easterner insists on the appearance of male-and-female."—Turkish/Syrian nightclub host and refugee **Mehmet Khouri**

"Madonna has an image of being pro-gay but her former pal Sandra Bernhard has said that in private she's not. You can't necessarily take an ex friend's word, but I heard more than once that during Madonna's marriage to that not-pro-gay British director she allegedly didn't invite her gay brother to their home. If that's so, then I can believe Bernhard, and the 'pro-gay' was a career strategy."—gay attorney **Tom Stockwell**

"Clark Gable was a gigolo whose first two wives were older and helped his career. The third, blonde movie star Carole Lombard, was after he became a star. She had gay male friends but during the marriage she converted to Gable's lifestyle. He loved hunting, his buddies were rednecks and he disliked gays intensely, possibly because he had a bisexual streak himself.

"Biographers say while Lombard was with Gable she set her gay friends aside... in deference to her husband's bigotry and insecurity."
—Hollywood historian **Lawrence J. Quirk**

"That kiss between Madonna and Britney Spears during an awards show was something else. I cheered. And kept waiting for a male version. In vain."
—singer/songwriter-producer **Michael Stipe**

"Women loved me in *My Best Friend's Wedding*. I think because women, unlike men, aren't obsessed with sex. Men tend to envy me because I'm tall and handsome. But when they find out I'm gay most of them dislike me. Women can think on more than one level."—**Rupert Everett**

"I logged on to my computer as a lesbian once. The lesbian chat rooms are pretty fun. Until you realize that every lesbian there is really a man trying to find a lesbian."—**Jon Lovitz**

"Grayson Hall received a supporting-Oscar nomination for playing a lesbian named Miss Fellowes in *The Night of the Iguana* [1964]. The script, not by Tennessee Williams but from his play, displayed lesbophobia... Ms. Hall was nominated partly for her courage in taking such a role, so long ago. And she was married and had a son, so... had she been single, she might not have been given that nomination."
—actress **Mary Grace Canfield** (Ralph the plumber on *Green Acres*)

"The police know plenty about some stars' private lives but they don't tell unless a crime occurs. For instance the police department near Katharine Hepburn's house, I think in Connecticut, used to get regular calls from neighbors when Kate and her genuine love Laura Harding, the American Express heiress, would drink too much nights and start fighting or carousing, throwing pots and pans around the kitchen."—**Erich Segal**, professor and novelist (*Love Story*)

"People could not conceive of male-female friendship, like that between Hepburn and alcoholic Spencer Tracy, whom she nursed [her father was a doctor]. They went around together, so people assumed they were sexual. It was said they lived together, without any evidence... Decades later, because Angelina Jolie and her then-closeted brother socialized and he kissed her when she won awards, people assumed...

"People need to get realistic, throw away the assumption that 'opposite sex' always means sex and same-sex almost never does."
—playwright **Edward Albee** (*A Delicate Balance*, whose film version starred Hepburn)

"Katharine Hepburn was so tremendously admired, and it showed in the biographies of her that kept closeting her even after her death. One of them by an openly gay writer related to the head of a major Hollywood talent agency. What that says to me is these writers—men writers—don't believe a lesbian can be admired. Excuse me? Ever heard of Florence Nightingale?"—publicist **Andrea Jaffe**

"At 15 my mother sent me to a psychiatrist because she thought I was a latent homosexual. There was nothing latent about it."—**Amanda Bearse** (*Married with Children*)

"I've always thought of David Cassidy as a latent heterosexual."—**Lil Smith**, editor of *Teen Bag* magazine

"I think memories of his father [actor Jack Cassidy] kept David in the closet. Like father, like son—bisexual. Shirley Jones, David's stepmom and Jack's ex, admits Jack was bi... Jack died in a fire, one of the worst ways to die... Even after David's career petered out—and by the way, he was *hung*—he avoided talking about his dad and about sexuality. He only mentioned girls."—**Mark X**, former production assistant on *The Partridge Family*

"Actors' egos... A few decades back a young movie star my age was in bed with me at his home near Santa Barbara. Enjoyable foreplay... then he said he wanted to 'fuck' me. Something new to me... I was tempted but didn't say yes or no. He was tipsy and I made it difficult for him to, uh, find entry. And he didn't.

"Turns out what he really wanted was me to screw him. But his movie-star ego didn't let him say so. Anyway, I did it and he loved it and when he came he yelled out so loud I thought maybe he was having a heart attack. And if so, what would the press say? But no. He was just expressing himself.

"He still hides behind the wife and kids. And the cult."—**George X**

"You know who they say is hung real good? I hear it from costumers and one of his brothers I know. Michael Jackson. What a waste, 'cause he doesn't put it to real use... Self-play, sometimes while he fondles boys... not even teenagers. I hear he prefers them pre-puberty."—**Howard Rollins Jr.** (*A Soldier's Story*)

"I was the one who first put [singer] Shaun Cassidy on an L.A. stage. But because I was gay his mother Shirley Jones thought I was fooling around with him. I wasn't, and he's straight and she's Republican. So we were professionally separated."
—former music promoter **David Forest**

"I directed Fred MacMurray more than once... when he fell to doing television, albeit successfully, and when I was through in motion pictures, I phoned him about being a director on his series [*My Three Sons*]. Fred apologized, said they'd already filled all the directing positions.

"My ass. I found out through a friend that Fred vetoed me on the basis of my being male-oriented... he was afraid for the boys playing those sons... I was *man*-oriented, not *boy*-oriented."—golden-age director **Mitchell Leisen**

"A few stars are so worried about publicity on them getting out or they're so afraid of AIDS that their computers are their whole sex lives. Other gay stars keep their sex-rated DVD's at the house of a friend or relative they really trust so in case they die sudden-like the incriminating stuff won't be found in their own homes. What a way to live, eh?"—publicist **Paul Bloch**

"Yeah, I get asked about that. You think I'm gonna be specific-like? I did. [Frequent] sex, yeah, with someone on the show. I liked it but it was always the same thing. I had to do it for him... You'll just have to *guess* who it could possibly be!"—**Ron Palillo** (*Welcome Back, Kotter*)

"There was much more terror of AIDS in the past, before it became a manageable condition instead of a death sentence. Now some go to the opposite extreme, ignoring safe sex altogether, since one can often survive 30 years after the diagnosis."
—**Richard Chamberlain** (*Dr. Kildare*)

"I feel invaded. That *Survivor* guy has stolen my name!"—actor **Richard Hatch** on the openly gay reality-series winner named Richard Hatch

"My pal, who started out as an actor, turns down all interview requests. He's cool with being gay. It's because most of each interview would be about his being HIV-positive and how his mother feels about it… in fact, all about his mother, period, since she's a star among stars. I mean, there's loads of guys would want to sleep with him just 'cause of who his mother is."
—**Steve X**, West Hollywood and Manhattan resident

"Until I played Alfred [the butler] on the television series *Batman* I never received interview requests to speak of. Only leading actors are sought for interviews… One female journalist inquired about my first marriage and I admitted I had been discouraged to find out she was a lesbian. The lady said, 'Oh, we can't print *that*.' Then why ask personal questions?"
—British actor **Alan Napier**

"Oscar Wilde was asked by an interviewer if he minded being asked an indiscreet question, and replied, 'My dear, there are no indiscreet questions—only indiscreet answers.' Don't you love it? Only, now nothing's indiscreet."—**Keira Knightley**

"I didn't write typical love stories. I didn't have helpless, smitten heroines falling into men's brawny arms. So a few journalists wondered aloud whether I had no personal interest in men?"—**Mildred Wirt Benson**, who created and wrote 23 Nancy Drew mystery novels

"I'm tall, I have a deep voice, sometimes I'm loud and argumentative. If that makes me a man, fine. I don't know that it makes me anything else."
—**Bea Arthur**

"All women have been sexually attracted to another woman... I can be attracted to a woman sexually."
—**Cameron Diaz**

"I'm wildly attracted to women. But I can understand why at given moments someone might think I'm homosexual... When I'm with a homosexual, I get a little homosexual. To make them feel at home, you see? I kind of camp a little. To bring them out. So they won't feel they're with a terrible straight."—**Orson Welles**

"Camping is fun! I don't mean where you sleep on the dirt and there's wild animals... But you have to be careful not to do it too often, or *where* you do it. Or people will label you queer... though I guess that's not the worst label. Better gay than someone who voted for Trump—that's an angry rump with a T in front of it."—comedian **Don Rickles**

"The lesbian magazine *Deneuve* was apparently named after Catherine Deneuve. She played a bisexual vampire in *The Hunger* and many lesbians find her ice-queen looks and image very appealing. Maybe less so after she sued the magazine—now called *Curve*. What I'd like to know is *how* she won that suit, since you cannot copyright a title or name. Or was it another case of homophobia trumps justice?"
—casting director **Barbara Dodd Remsen**

"Our Italian actresses are genuine beauties. Some of them even have personalities. I have found myself staring for minutes at a time at photos of some of them... a strange fascination that is envy and unearned admiration with a sandwich layer of desire that I cannot rationally explain."—journalist and author **Oriana Fallaci**

"If a straight guy admits to himself that another guy is good-looking, he usually stops himself, afraid it might mean he's sexually attracted. As opposed to just admitting an esthetic fact... Patriarchal society does its best to make and keep heterosexual men insecure."
—producer **Craig Zadan**

"On several levels, we lived in terror. The police were fucking fascists, free to act like terrorists against gay men, even to invading their homes and arresting them on trumped-up 'morals' charges... Henry Willson was the unscrupulous agent of Rock Hudson, Tab Hunter, Robert Wagner and others. He was known to sexually audition potential actor clients. Okay, that was part of the casting couch. But quite unforgivably, this gay man sometimes blackmailed actor clients he'd had sex with."—former actor **Jack Larson**

"I had rather a bit of a crush on a boy in elementary school. It terrified me... until years later when I became convinced I really did like girls."
—former James Bond **Roger Moore**

"I think at some time in every girl's life there's another girl in school whom you cannot cease admiring. She's bright, she's funny, her socks are just right and if she chooses to walk down the hall with you, you float. And that's a crush, and girls have crushes on other girls in school."—**Victoria Principal** (*Dallas*)

"Do I like women? I like women. Do I like them sexually? Yeah, I do. Totally."—**Drew Barrymore**

"I never said I like women that way. What I've said is I like being something like a man. I had a strong role in *Giant*—an admirably butch character. In *The Exorcist* I was the voice of the devil. I broke the silence and revealed that I was that voice. They weren't going to give me any credit! Oh, I've had an unusual career."—**Mercedes McCambridge**, who had a small male role in Orson Welles's *Touch of Evil*

"Hey, it's one reason I always wear a little ribbon in my hair. I mean, just because I was on *The Dick Van Dyke Show*..."—**Rose Marie**

"Am I gay? Ha, ha, ha, aah... go ahead. Ask me anything you want. Clitoral or vaginal? Both, darling. I'll take anything I can get. Hah!"—**Valerie Harper**

"I'd hate for anyone to think of me as a big butch lady."—tall closeted British singer **Dusty Springfield**

"I don't know how the rumor got started that we were a couple. Whatever it is we each are in our private lives is something we each keep private. But a couple... we were not a couple. Maybe someone just liked the idea of two beautiful women together."
—**Julie Christie** on rumors that linked her with model Lauren Hutton

"We're a couple. Yes… just don't ask me how long it'll last. How long does anything last? It's how good it is that counts."—**Lindsay Lohan**, during her relationship with deejay Samantha Ronson

"Why hasn't Sean Hayes come out? Maybe he's afraid of being stereotyped as gay stereotypes. I hope he comes out. The actor who plays Will is openly straight. The actor who plays Jack should be openly gay."—anonymous **producer** of *Will and Grace* (Hayes finally did come out)

"There's almost as much variation among women-loving women as there is among left-handed people. However, stereotypes stand out and the media dwells on them. So you don't notice or know the majority of lesbians and bisexuals."
—**Amanda Bearse** (*Married with Children*)

"I consider myself bisexual."—**Megan Mullally** (*Will and Grace*)

"Any woman that says she never thought about lesbian sex is lying."—**Kristy Swanson** (*Buffy the Vampire Slayer*)

"I wouldn't be surprised if I ended up with a woman… It seems we're all bisexual, if you want to get kind of simple about it."—**Lili Taylor** (*I Shot Andy Warhol*)

"We're both bisexual and it's beautiful."—French actress **Maria Schneider** on herself and *Last Tango in Paris* costar Marlon Brando (she'd also included

Tango director Bernardo Bertolucci, who asked her to "take it back")

"I'm bisexual and comfortable with saying that. Older generations weren't even comfortable saying they were heterosexual. Sex, period, made them uncomfortable. I'm glad I wasn't born earlier than I was."—**Andy Dick**

"… The fastest-growing population in the world."—**Mick Jagger**'s 1970s description of bisexuals

"I'm curious why when a woman admits she's bisexual people believe her. But when a man—of course they do it much less often—says he's bisexual, often he's not believed." —**Kate Winslet**

"In spirit… Probably."—**Kurt Cobain**'s answers to the questions "Are you gay?" and "Are you bisexual?" (In school his best friend was gay and got gay-bashed, as did Cobain for having a gay friend.)

"I certainly wasn't real confident with girls. I guess that's what got me started with guys. And small animals."—TV hunk **Jon-Erik Hexum** (1957-1984) to *Playgirl* magazine, which officially claimed a readership of heterosexual females

"Sure! Hasn't everyone?"
—hunk actor **Scott Valentine**, when asked if he'd had gay experiences

"While he was in France shooting *Last Tango in Paris* Marlon Brando revealed that he'd had homosexual experiences in his life and was unashamed. Bravo. But why did his movie feature a gratuitous and violent anti-gay scene? Its director, Bernardo Bertolucci, was gay or bi... Come to think of it, he's the one who pretended *The Last Emperor* was straight, although the real emperor wasn't... and then, for falsifying the historical truth Bertolucci won a Best Director Oscar."—critic **Ron Franzone**

"Garbo was able to get away with a kissing scene with an actress in *Queen Christina* in 1933, though mostly the picture presented the Swedish monarch as straight... Garbo was willing to come out of retirement to costar with Marilyn Monroe in a female version of *The Picture of Dorian Gray*. Marilyn was willing, the financiers weren't."—Sir **Cecil Beaton**, three-time Oscar-winning set and costume designer

"I discovered Dr. Anna Freud's findings when she analyzed Marilyn during a week in London in 1956. According to Anna [daughter of Sigmund Freud], Marilyn was bisexual."—Dr. **Lois Banner**, MM biographer

"A man who had kissed me once said it was very possible I was a lesbian because I apparently had no response to males—meaning him. I didn't contradict him because I didn't know what I was."—**Marilyn Monroe**

"Natasha [Lytess, acting coach] was with Marilyn almost from her career's inception. Their relationship ran from 1948 to 1953, the year Marilyn's superstardom was confirmed at the box office. During those years Natasha helped Marilyn to gain confidence and gave her the tools to act… After Marilyn broke through big-time, pressure was applied to drop Natasha for the sake of Marilyn's image and her long-term acceptance by Middle America."—psychologist Dr. **Betty Berzon**

"Monroe lived with her lesbian coach part of the time and drove the man directors crazy because when a scene was completed Marilyn would turn to the woman for approval, not the director. Those guys were envious and angry… In later years Marilyn used [coach] Lee Strasberg's wife instead."—actress **Sheree North**, hired as a "threat" to MM

"Of the umpteen actresses who've played Marilyn Monroe or dyed their hair to look more like her, I'd say most have wanted to be her—before she died—or wanted to *have* her… and who wouldn't?"—casting director **Ingrid Gibson**

"RuPaul knew it had to be blonde hair. If his wig was dark-haired his illusion wouldn't be one-eighth as effective… He's fooled several hetero guys who didn't know who he was. That can be dangerous. The guy who insists he's '100 percent straight' often isn't completely sure."—writer **E. Lynn Harris**

"I was approached by more than one famous actress in my heyday. Usually brunettes. I wasn't lesbian but my impression is brunette women who prefer women go after blondes… I did have a crush on

Marilyn Monroe. I would never have said no to her, and any reasonable husband would understand that!"—blonde **Gloria Stuart** (*Titanic*)

"Most sexually realistic women know better than to say 'never.'"—**Anna Nicole Smith**

"Women can take a compliment. From anyone, young, old, male, female. It's men who aren't reared to be gracious or confident in their looks."—**Madonna**

"I would love to be someone's lesbian crush."
—**Jane Fonda**

"What's not to be flattered? After a certain age you're grateful anyone still finds you sexy."
—**Joan Rivers**

"Straight men dislike the idea of being gay. I don't think women much mind the female-female concept, but most dislike the word. 'Lesbian' seems an unfeminine word. 'Sapphic' is better, but no one knows what it means. And it rhymes with traffic."—straight UK actress **Jean Simmons** (*Guys and Dolls, Spartacus*)

"I wouldn't mind being called a gay woman if it didn't sound like somebody tipsy. Or drunk. I'm a teetotaler… I would not want to be called that other word [lesbian]. It sounds like someone from a communist country."—**Marjorie Main**, aka Ma Kettle

"The Americans came up with 'straight' to mean heterosexual. To me, 'straight' means honest, and I'm

now straight about being gay—or lesbian. I don't think most heterosexual women are straight about their capacity for sexual pleasure from both genders."
—British character actor **Miriam Margolyes** (Harry Potter's Professor Pomona Sprout)

"Anglo and Anglo-American culture are very down on men having feelings, preferring them to hide their feelings. Eventually my father came out to me, and I was relieved for him."—actor **Corin Redgrave** on Sir Michael Redgrave

"I'm glad I'm Latino. We hug and touch. We express affection for both genders and non-relatives too. This makes it much easier when you happen to be gay, which I am."—comedian **Frank Maya**

"Britain is less puritanical than the States, which was founded by Puritans... Sir Noel Coward didn't come out officially but he did not hide behind a wife as Cole Porter did, and both were extremely successful... Barry Manilow is allegedly gay but remains in the closet, while Sir Elton John's coming out made him bigger than ever."—**Lynn Redgrave** (Manilow has since come out)

"I don't get it about Manilow being so closeted. He did a single acting job, a TV movie, of course playing straight. But he's a singer, not a screen lover. And deep into middle age, it's bizarre to still be hiding."—female impressionist (Judy Garland, Barbra Streisand) **Jim Bailey**

"In England there was Danny La Rue, a nationally famous female impersonator. Life-long closet case. In this country Jim Bailey refused ever to state his sexual orientation. If they're ashamed to be gay, choose a less obvious line of work! Like a truck driver or a butcher."—**Robin Leach**, host of TV's *Lifestyles of the Rich and Famous*

"The producers of *The Brady Bunch* worried that Alice, the family housekeeper—and the actress playing her [Ann B. Davis]—wasn't frilly-femmy enough. So they gave her a boyfriend—a butcher!"
—TV writer **Susan Watanabe**

"Well, they had Jethro for Miss Jane [Hathaway on *The Beverly Hillbillies*, played by Nancy Kulp]. It ain't working. Then they had the butcher for Alice, but who was butcher than Alice?"—openly gay comedian **Suzanne Westenhoefer** on feeble attempts to closet lesbian sitcom characters

"My definition of ridiculous? One is: a closeted fashion designer. In Europe most of us are out. In the USA many or most are inside. Some do come out after the wrinkles appear, like Calvin Klein. Do those men think people cannot guess about the average fashion designer?"—**Karl Lagerfeld**

"The average public has no idea how ordinary a gay man can be. They aren't all hairdressers, decorators, actors, etc. Gays are in every profession, from garbage collectors and sports to whatever's the opposite of flamboyant."—openly gay actor **Cheyenne Jackson** (*American Horror Story*)

"I must say that the general public's impression that either there are very few gay people or they start out straight and 'choose' to be gay is due primarily to gay people's silence and, in past generations more so, cowardice."—gay UK actor **Michael Cashman**

"An invisible minority is a discriminated-against minority. I know, *twice*… I'm Hispanic —*Life* magazine called us 'the invisible minority' decades ago, and we still don't speak up. I'm also gay, and we're finally—some of us—speaking up."—comedian **Consuelo Martin**

"The wheel that squeaks loudest gets the grease. Harvey Fierstein says it's too bad gay people can't be physically identified, like blacks, that if we could be, we'd have to stand up for ourselves and not shrink back in silence or pretend to be someone else."—actor and sci-fi novelist (gay-themed *Chrome*) **George Nader**

"If we don't define ourselves, others will define us, incorrectly and negatively. They'll even write lots of lies about what we do in bed, as David Reuben did with the gay material in his bestselling book *Everything You Always Wanted to Know About Sex… But Were Afraid to Ask*."—actor **Terry Lester** (*The Young and the Restless*)

"I witnessed how the tabloids dealt with gays when a young actor I knew came down with AIDS-related illnesses. Because at the time he was well known for playing a heartthrob on a daytime soap, he became a prime object of tabloid scrutiny. Photographers dogged his every step. Reporters camped outside his door. All this, as he fought and finally succumbed to the terrible deterioration that HIV can bring."—**Lance Loud**, the openly gay son in the pioneering 1970s PBS reality series *An American Family*

"The dumber the reader, the less progressive... I knew a top tabloid editor who admitted their office building's janitor was gay, his gardener was gay and his dentist was gay. But he had a policy of not admitting that dull, ordinary men could be gay. Otherwise, he said, it would threaten his readership."—**Rick X**, magazine editor and former tabloid editor

"In real life Liberace liked them rough. Football players, chauffeurs from the wrong side of the tracks... Publicly, he said he lost his virginity to an older woman. Her name was Miss Bea Haven."
—Sir **Elton John**

"[Male] actors aren't that romantic on screen. So when Cary Grant came on to me I was surprised. But those actresses who died for love, like Greta Garbo—I was dumbfounded when I found out she was gay. All those wonderful love scenes! Of course then you catch on what a wonderful actress she was."—fashion designer and critic **Mr. Blackwell**

"Sophia Loren got lots of mileage out of her story about a pseudo-affair with costar Cary Grant. When her memoir included it, Grant was privately livid but publicly didn't contradict her. He felt it was a gross distortion and invasion of his privacy but it did depict him as straight and if he'd objected people might wonder why, since any straight man was expected to go ape over Sophia."—reviewer **Brian Handler**

"It's weird. Women are so much more selective with women than they are with men."
—**Drew Barrymore**

"There's a whole bunch of wives of famous gay men, straight women who had prior relationships with straight men that turned out badly... as in physical abuse. That was the case with Cole Porter's wife Linda and it's the case with the actress wife of a star who's had kids with her but goes from one male lover to another despite all his 'family' publicity."—talent manager and producer **Sandy Gallin**

"If a woman came into my life who was absolutely stunning and satisfied me emotionally, intellectually and sexually, I'm not going to draw the line and say, 'I can't, because you're a woman.' I find it hard enough to find someone to be with, why narrow the field?"—British actress **Amanda Donohoe** (*L.A. Law*)

"Anthony Perkins was gay but unhappy. He'd have been unhappy, regardless. I knew him. At 40 he married a woman—gay or bi, who can know for sure? He began preaching about the joys of straight marriage. He didn't stop having anonymous gay sex. Died of AIDS. She's gone too."—screenwriter **Robert Getchell**

"Vladek Sheybal was an unusual-looking but handsome actor of Polish origin. An eccentric. He confided in me that when he masturbated he wore a glove so he couldn't give himself AIDS."—Britisher **Ken Russell**, who directed Sheybal in *Women in Love* and *The Boyfriend*

"You'd think music celebrities who aren't actors or heartthrobs would be more open... but not necessarily. Like one gay guy, half of a sister-brother act. She died, so that was it for him. Came from conservative parents, so now he's married, several kids, likes to say marriage and fatherhood is the *only* way to live."—openly gay composer **Lesley Gore** ("Out Here on My Own")

"The closet is akin to a vertical coffin."—director **John Schlesinger**

"I know Michael, he likes real young guys, also blonds, also muscular guys. But not guys like me... I think he's spending too much time with underaged boys. If he thinks they're less likely to tell, that's dumb. Some boys go and tell their parents stuff."
—poet **Essex Hemphill**

"The D.A. has decided not to press charges against Michael Jackson. He can stop pretending to be married to Lisa Marie [Presley] now."—**Jay Leno** during a 1994 *Tonight Show* monologue

"Michael [Jackson] did a song titled 'Muscles' about bodybuilders' sexy bodies. But Diana Ross sang it... He tries to hide behind innocence. *Esquire* magazine said he did a private calendar posing as a scoutmaster surrounded by pre-adolescent boys."
—**Peter Lieberson**, composer son of Columbia Records mogul Goddard Lieberson

"No, no. He didn't write that song about me. I heard he wrote it about Cary Grant."
—**Douglas Fairbanks Jr.** on Noel Coward's song "Mad About the Boy"

"He [the Duke of Windsor, former king of England] pretends not to hate me, but he does, and it's because I'm queer and he's queer but unlike him I don't pretend not to be."—Sir **Noel Coward** to Truman Capote, according to Coward biographer Clive Fisher

"I knew Sid Grauman, a confirmed bachelor if ever there was one. He was very publicity-shy. However in that time period reporters didn't inquire into a public figure's private life. Sid would be horrified today."—producer and "toastmaster general" **George Jessel** on the closeted real estate magnate behind Grauman's Chinese and Egyptian theatres

"The proverbial bachelor uncle gets routinely teased by relatives at family get-togethers with 'Still haven't found the right girl yet?' If only more men would say, 'I'm not looking for one.'

"I had a wonderful gay uncle. He congratulated me when I came out. But it's as if entire generations were unable, were paralyzed... I'm not criticizing, it's just hard to comprehend why it took so many, many centuries for any sort of gay rights and gay voice to come into existence."—**Melissa Etheridge**

"Is there any doubt that for some 2,000 years religion has held gay people down? I speak of the religions born in the Middle East—Judaism and its two offspring, Christianity and then Islam. Like the landscape they all came from, those are hard religions."—**Truman Capote**

"I grew up in Jamestown, New York, where Lucille Ball did... When I came out to my mother she asked, 'Are you going to be promoting homosexuality?' Like *they* never promote heterosexuality... but I said to her, 'No, I'll be recruiting.'"—**Mitchell Anderson**, the violin teacher on *Party of Five*

"Bob Hope was a vastly popular and vastly overrated comic actor for decades. He had two openly lesbian daughters, also a nephew who died of AIDS. All he ever talked about was himself... Someone finally asked about his family and he said something like, if they were interesting they'd be celebrities and tell their own stories."—**Tommy Kirk** (*Babes in Toyland, The Absent-Minded Professor*)

(In a NYC cab, in the middle of stopped traffic, with a van driver staring at him) "The fellow turned to his friend, then leaned out the window and yelled, 'Hey, faggot!' It was really a horrific moment. I just sat there and thought, 'Well, here's the flip side of fame.'" —**Nathan Lane** in 1996, to *Time* magazine, whose 1998 75th anniversary issue completely excluded gay people

"My hometown [Monroeville, Alabama] was so provincial, if a boy said he wanted to be an actor, that was tantamount to coming out."
—**Truman Capote**

"The media idealizes small towns, like Mayberry. That's fiction. In the real world small town normally means small-minded... and the smaller the mind, the bigger the homophobia. It's cities that afford gay people protection. Though in Hollywood's case that's debatable."—**Divine** (*Pink Flamingoes*)

"People forget that [in the early 20th century] most heterosexual couples did not necessarily get legally married. In 19th-century England most were not... One of the biggest reasons, apart from straight propaganda, that nearly every Hollywood movie ended with a new about-to-marry girl and boy was to encourage all heterosexuals to marry—to join the system. A system of controlled behavior."—historian **Carlos Clarens**

"Hollywood rewards good looks, regardless what's inside. How many people used to assume Mel Gibson was a peach of a guy? I remember an old movie, *A Woman's Face* [starring Joan Crawford, directed by George Cukor], where the woman is scarred, so she's a villain. Until a plastic surgeon removes her scar, then suddenly she's a peach... I'm afraid Hollywood's 'values' are, excuse the pun, pretty superficial."—*Let's Make a Deal* host and film buff **Monty Hall**

"If you're pretty and male and young like, say, Zac Efron or Justin Bieber, rumors crop up about your private life. Are you gay? Are you bi? Kinky? What else? People are interested—till you lose your looks. This happens to most young hunks. People pin their fantasies or kinks onto them, regardless."—openly gay actor **Danny Pintauro** (*Who's the Boss*)

"It's true that the latest hunk actor in town is often whispered to be sexually fluid. Often or usually it's untrue. But—big but—if the whispers and rumors persist... if 10, 20 or 30 years later they're still saying it, whether he's married to a woman or not, well, where there's smoke there's usually fire."—**Peggy Feury**, acting coach to Tom Cruise, Lily Tomlin and others

"Brad Pitt is to my knowledge straight. But he did live with a gay man, an older man, for a while. That fact has disappeared from his bio and from his conversation with interviewers... I think because any pretty boy is suspected of going either way. Many do, either for fun or for their career. But very few admit it later."
—**Wayne Warga**, head writer for *Entertainment Tonight*

"As actresses age they become less generally feminine, their voices deeper... Lucille Ball, Bette Davis, etc. Some non-straight men like Vincent Price become more queeny. In middle age Price was lucky to move from supporting actor to leading man—but leads in horror movies. Despite, or because of, his queeniness they'd put a younger woman next to him in his movies' ads."—theatrical executive **Dwight Frye Jr.**, whose father appeared in *Dracula* and *Frankenstein*

"Vincent Price's daughter Victoria came out about herself but only hinted about her father in her book... In later years he married the English actress Coral Browne and they became best friends. But I think it was to camouflage himself… and maybe her too."—talk-radio host **Lynn Samuels**

"Tyne Daly [*Cagney and Lacey*] won't admit that her father James Daly [*Medical Center*] was gay and had a male lover whom she and her sisters evicted from [the men's] apartment after James Daly died."
—**Howard Ashman**, producer and Oscar-winning lyricist (*The Little Mermaid*)

"Tyne Daly was asked if she had any gay relatives and replied that that was a terrible question. It's her attitude that's terrible. Hopefully she's come around since then."—**Ed Asner**

"Elizabeth Taylor might never have gone to Hollywood but for her father's lover. Victor Cazalet was a wealthy Member of Parliament. As World War II approached, he arranged for Francis, whom he loved, and his wife and little boy and girl to leave England for the United States. Elizabeth would otherwise have continued growing up in England and probably become a wife and society hostess. Her ambitious actress mother gave up the stage when she married Francis."—ET's gay secretary **Roger Wall**

"Kirk Douglas had four sons and, as is often the case, the youngest was gay. Eric was bipolar and apparently a suicide. Mr. Douglas, now over 100, has difficulty admitting Eric was gay. Perhaps at that age we can excuse him. I say no more."—photographer **Larry Jeffers**, friend of Eric Douglas

"Word is, Prince Edward was pushed into marrying by Prince Philip [his father]... I'd feel sorry for him except he gets to live off the fat of the land's people and when everyone was asking if he were gay, he pronounced that an 'insult' to his family!... I'm not gay but I've visited a gay pub in London called The Queen's Youngest Son."—director **Ken Russell**

"My son David was the first AIDS Coordinator in Los Angeles. In his memory, I'm participating in several fundraisers to help stop AIDS... Those who believe AIDS is God's punishment believe in a devil, not a god. How do they explain the Black Death that killed off a third of Europe?"—**Russell Johnson**, the Professor on *Gilligan's Island*

"I have three sons, I dearly love them all. [But] my gay son is the apple of my eye."—**Sally Field**

"I don't have a son, and one kid is plenty. Princess Di said if men could have children, no man would ever have more than one... But I'm hoping to have a gay grandson. Yes! What, do you think a straight grandson would ever come and visit me except to ask for money? Or an audition? And gay sons don't dump their mothers for a wife and kids and hookers on the side and I've-been-meaning-to-call-I'm-just-so-busy, yakety-yak-yak-yak. Feh!"—**Joan Rivers**

"Richard [Pryor] goes both ways. He publicly admitted he'd gone down on a guy at a benefit he did with Bette Midler and Lily Tomlin... Richard Pryor Jr. is a cross-dresser. Richard Sr. is cool about it. He says little Richard is still his son even if he dresses like his daughter. But big Richard got kind of upset when he found out his son was performing in drag in Peoria. I don't blame him. I mean, Peoria!"—family friend **LeVon August**

"The openly lesbian daughter of Lana Turner, Cheryl Crane, is a successful realtor and novelist, and very pretty. As a teenager she bravely and fatally stabbed mobster Johnny Stompanato, Lana's lover, who was violent and threatening to disfigure Lana's face."—gay producer **Allan Carr** (*Grease*), who hoped to film Crane's memoir, *Detour*

"Marlon Brando was the first American superstar to come out as bisexual. But don't expect him to confess that one of his late son's male lovers was Marlon's lover, first."—talk show host **Skip E. Lowe**

"James Mason and wife were long rumored to be in a ménage-a-trois with a policeman. All his life Mason had to relegate his true sexuality to the shadows. I think he would be proud that his grandson James Duke Mason, an actor and aspiring Democratic politician, is openly gay. James Mason's son had campaigned, ironically, for Ronald Reagan."—gay historian **Shelley Powell**

"I could be killed if I went to Egypt because my father married a Jewish woman and I am gay."
—**Omar Sharif Jr.**, grandson of the actor born Michel Shalhoub (a Lebanese surname) who married an Egyptian movie star, converted to Islam and became

an Egyptian star until *Lawrence of Arabia* brought international fame

"For gay people in the 1950s this was practically a police state. You could be arrested in your own home if you had an all-male pajama party. If one person had a marijuana cigarette, the whole crowd was arrested. If you got hold of an X-rated movie reel you could be arrested, even if you viewed it alone.

"You weren't allowed to dance in a gay bar or touch another man there. Gays couldn't be depicted on stage then. If you 'loitered' anywhere and seemed gay, you'd be arrested. Not to mention public restrooms—you could be innocent, but if you were inside one and a cop wanted to, he'd arrest you for 'lewdness' or 'public indecency.'

"How it ever got to that awful point I don't know. But some of it happened to me."—**Tab Hunter**

"Anderson Cooper's grandmother was lesbian, which his mother Gloria Vanderbilt has admitted. As a child Gloria was taken away from the care of her 'unfit' mother, who had an affair with Lord Mountbatten's sister-in-law. Mountbatten, the last British ruler of India, was himself rumored to be gay. His wife Edwina reportedly had an affair with Nehru, India's first prime minister."—historian **Fergus Warnock**

"Sports figures often aren't the best fathers to gay or HIV-positive sons. Dodgers manager Tommy Lasorda didn't acknowledge the AIDS death of Tommy Lasorda Jr., who officially died of 'pneumonia volume depletion.' By contrast, theatrical producer

Joseph Papp acknowledged his son's death from AIDS and took part in AIDS fundraising activities, which Lasorda did not."—sports blogger **Steward Hill**

"… died after a long illness."—*Variety*, "the showbiz bible," not clarifying the AIDS death of Nat King Cole's son (and Natalie Cole's brother) Nat Kelly Cole, a writer, at 36 in 1995

"He was a fine actor and human being. He will be missed."—**Leonard Nimoy**, aka Mr. Spock, on Merritt Butrick, who played Captain Kirk's son in the films *Star Trek II* and *III* and died of AIDS at 29 in 1989

"Johnny Carson Shattered as Gay Son Dies of AIDS"—**1994 *Globe* tabloid headline** about Carson's stepson, only child of ex-wife Joanna Carson, in whose home Truman Capote had died ten years earlier

"Family Heartbreak… After 8 Wives and 11 Children… Mickey Rooney's Agony: His Son Is Secret Gay!"—**1992 *Globe* tabloid headline** (the son's mother, Rooney's fifth wife, was shot dead by her heterosexual male lover)

"So Hollywood's two leading gossip columnists, Louella Parsons and Hedda Hopper, were homophobes. Each woman had one child. Each child was homosexual." —biographer **Lawrence J. Quirk** (Harriet Parsons produced such films as *I Remember Mama*; actor William Hopper costarred on TV's *Perry Mason* and may have been a lover of its star Raymond Burr)

"My favorite nephew is gay. He is one of the leaders in Norway in AIDS activism and I'm very proud of him... I did not know at the time that I was one of the first of not at all enough celebrities in America who denounced Anita Bryant and her mission of hate against the gay citizens of that country."—**Liv Ullmann**

"We've made inquiries but received no response from Martin Sheen [born Ramon Estevez] about his gay porn star nephew Brian Estevez, who starred in *The Young and* the *Hung*... Brian is the spitting image of the young Martin."—X-rated-films distributor **Adam Block**

"Rita Hayworth has been criticized for switching from Margarita Cansino to a more WASP-y image. Why? Her mother was Irish and Rita chose her mother's last name. It made sense professionally and still makes sense personally. We're biologically more a part of our mothers than our fathers, and mothers do most of the child-rearing. Instead, criticize unscrupulous actors who still marry a woman as a stepping stone."
—gay comedian **Frank Maya** (Hayworth's gay grandson committed suicide)

"Joan hated her brother... not because he was bisexual. He was alcoholic and very much their mother's favorite. Also lazy. After Joan got him a studio job they finally fired him."—**Cesar Romero**, friend and platonic escort of Joan Crawford

"Gay stars from Charles Laughton to Johnny Mathis have had gay brothers they don't talk about.

But that's because: a) celebs aren't encouraged to discuss siblings, only their mates, kids and sometimes parents, b) a sibling may bitterly resent being talked about and c) some sibs do want to be talked about—lots!—so they can become semi celebrities." —openly gay actor **Louis Edmonds** (*Dark Shadows*)

"I come from a gay family."—Spanish-language talk show host **Cristina Saralegui** at the 2000 GLAAD (Gay & Lesbian Alliance Against Defamation) awards show, referring to her lesbian sister and gay brother

"Roseanne Barr has a gay brother and a lesbian sister… At times she sounds pro-gay but she also uses anti-gay language, and sometimes she's supportive of her siblings but other times she's estranged. She's peculiar in her outlooks and inconsistency."—paddle-ball maestro **Reggie Rymal** (*House of Wax*)

"Since entertainers are often looked up to, I think it's a responsibility to do what we can to lessen the hatred and misconceptions. That's why I've written pro-gay lyrics, on account of Betsy."—country singer **Garth Brooks** about his openly lesbian sister

"I remember one time I scratched this girl's back in the middle of the night. I was nine and she was 12 and she asked me to scratch her back. A nun ran in, ripped me off her back, threw me against the lockers, beat the shit out of me and called me a lesbian. I didn't know what a lesbian was."—singer **Cyndi Lauper**, who acknowledges her openly gay sister

"[Katharine] Hepburn had a homosexual brother. He died young, perhaps suicide... the topic was taboo but she took his birth date for her own—she only corrected the record toward the end of her life... I can tell you Miss Hepburn was not pro-gay—not toward gay men, anyway."—actor **Fritz Feld**, husband of Virginia Christine, who appeared in *Guess Who's Coming to Dinner*

"My brother said he had cancer and my family wanted it known he died of that. But it's important folks should know what's killing who... 'cause we have got to do something about this, even if one effing president after another doesn't want to do anything unless he's fucking forced."—**Nell Carter** (*Gimme a Break*), who announced that her gay brother had died of AIDS

"I love and fully support my gay brother Eamon, who because of his difference was a victim of bullying and violence. This is unacceptable in Ireland, and it is unacceptable everywhere. Gay men are our brothers, literally."—**Colin Farrell**

"Asinine! Angelina Jolie's cute brother went to industry functions with her and they'd kiss on the lips, as some family members do... like Kirk Douglas and his son Michael. But with a girl and boy, so many people whispered *incest*? Didn't anyone think *platonic* and maybe he's gay? At least he later came out, so that settled that."—**Tab Hunter**

"Oh, I do have relatives more romantically drawn to their own genders. I'd be willing to talk about them, they're wonderful people, all my family is interesting. But

I don't dare get them in any trouble." —movie and TV star **Robert Cummings** (whose physician father's patient and friend was Orville Wright, Robert's godfather)

"Not too often, a homophobic celebrity's career does suffer. This singer whose name is unknown to younger people went on the warpath against gay people and it backfired on her. It was not popularly known that a driving motivation was that she discovered her husband was gay or bisexual. He continued hiding behind her big skirts and cross religion. Wherever she is now, she should only stay there."—screenwriter and AMPAS president **Fay Kanin**

"I suspected [new husband] Warde was 'bi' from day one, but his looks kept bringing me back… and he was a nice guy—when he was sober… We arrived in Australia. At the airport I was given a chauffeur and a limo. They dropped me off at the hotel, then Warde and the chauffeur went to the beach… When Warde got back I knew he'd blown the guy because he had semen on his breath."—**Phyllis Diller**, who detailed her dud marriages in her memoir *Like a Lampshade in a Whorehouse*

"I've finally found peace and happiness with my second husband."—**Vivian Vance** (*I Love Lucy*) on publisher John Dodds, who was her fourth husband and gay

"People are talking about you and Lucy, you ought to be careful about the hugging and kissing you do on the show. You behave like a couple of dykes in heat."
—Vivian Vance's third husband, actor **Phil Ober**, who appeared on *I Love Lucy*

"Carol's husband was a handsome man, he swept her off her feet. He produced her TV show and was, or became, alcoholic. He was bisexual. They divorced... One of Carol's three daughters is openly bisexual, and Carol [Burnett] is all for gay rights and campaigned for the failed Equal Rights Amendment that the Republicans torpedoed."—columnist **Susan Leda**

"Joanie's first husband, the actor Maxwell Reed, was a character. His laugh was a high-pitched shriek. Though he looked gruff his voice was occasionally squeaky, so he learned to keep his chin down to produce deeper vocal sounds... He disliked his wife using his mascara because he would put it under the tap but she would spit into it... A few years later their divorce was especially acrimonious."—**Roger Moore**, former James Bond, on friend Joan Collins

"Before she married into Pepsi Cola, Joan Crawford had three actor husbands. All were bisexual. She cheated on the second one, movie star Franchot Tone, but he cheated on her with Bette Davis and Ross Alexander."—British biographer **David Bret**

"Carol Channing has had four husbands. The happiest marriage was the last, but he died too soon. The unhappy third one lasted longer than the rest put together, about 42 years. Charles Lowe became his wife's utterly domineering manager. He was a closeted gay who was openly anti-gay. Who knows why, but he divorced her, then tried to sue her for implying he was gay... Carol's memoirs made no mention of him whatsoever."—reviewer **John Pulleyblank**

"Being a 'royal' isn't a joy. Look at the queen's sister. Princess Margaret was in love, but he wasn't enough of a blue-blood. She was married off to Anthony Armstrong-Jones, aka Lord Snowdon. Only insiders wondered... but after the divorce *Chic* magazine wrote, 'Class-conscious matchmakers can't help hoping for a more fitting liaison in the future, perhaps between Snowdon and fellow consort of sorts Prince Henrik of Denmark.'"—**Martin Greif**, author of *The Gay Book of Days*

"Michael Korda, head of Simon & Schuster [publishers], wrote a novel called *Queenie* that sold like hotcakes. Its real shocker was about the Laurence Olivier-Danny Kaye affair. Many people didn't believe it because they seemed such an odd couple. Like Rock Hudson and Gomer Pyle, that is, Jim Nabors."—columnist **Gay Boy Ric**

"If you worry too much about what the public thinks, you are no longer an artist, you are a salesman."—French movie star **Alain Delon**, who nonetheless sued a newspaper that said he was bisexual

"I did support myself in style via prostitution before I became a successful actor. It's not at all unusual—for an actor or an actress—to have done that. What is extraordinarily unusual is to admit it."
—**Rupert Everett** (*The Importance of Being Earnest*)

"The men I had sex with [for money] were *nice* to me... They were the only people who found me attractive, sexy and worthwhile. Girls were not nice to me! And even though I wasn't turned on by it, I have only deep love for the gay men I was close with—filmmakers and artists and brilliant men... How could I be homophobic about those experiences? I guess I'm not insecure in that way."—**Vincent Gallo** (*Truth or Consequences, NM*)

"If you work around ordinary-looking people, you're straight or you're gay. Okay? If you work around actors, actresses, models—male or female—you're potentially bisexual. The more attractive people are, the more tempted anyone's gonna be."—male supermodel **Joe MacDonald**

"Fuck Helmut Newton [the photographer]. Why should I take my clothes off for him? I took my clothes off for his wife."—**Janice Dickinson**, 1970s supermodel

"There is a double standard of Hollywood that apparently is seldom discussed in that country. It is the near nudity and complete nudity so common to actresses on the screen, but the very seldom even partial nudity of the actors. To see a penis you must see a French or other European film."—openly gay French star **Jean-Claude Brialy**

"I believe Viggo Mortensen is heterosexual... doesn't matter—*we* don't discriminate against *them*... He's done a film [*Eastern Promises*] in which he appears very utterly nude... in an extended, violent fight scene on what looks like a tile floor. Even so, *that* DVD is a guaranteed seller among the brethren."—**Alec McCowen** (*Travels with My Aunt*)

"Weirdly enough, girls ask less questions than guys do. Guys want to know everything about it, like, 'What? How much? When? Were you naked?'"
—**Channing Tatum** (*Magic Mike*) on reaction to his having been a male stripper in real life

"If you ask who I live with, what or who appeals to me, those are not terribly personal questions. If you inquire what I think of in order to obtain a particular emotional response while acting, that is personal."
—gay actor **Roscoe Lee Brown**

"I've always said it's not necessarily who you have sex with that defines your sexuality. Closeted gay men can and do have sex with their wives and straight men in prison can and do have sex with men and enjoy it... The backbone of your sexuality is who you fall in love with, who you have crushes on, who you fantasize about while you're having sex with whoever you're stuck with at the moment."—**Christopher Isherwood**

"If a couple of any sexual stripe is mutually honest, they may ask each other post-coitus, 'I'll tell you who I was thinking about if you'll tell me who you were thinking about.'"—**Gore Vidal**, who dedicated his novel *Myra Breckinridge* to Christopher Isherwood

"Heterosexual men are surprisingly insecure... forever trying to make boys grow up to be 'straight,' mostly through sports, endlessly screening male-female kisses and pairing off males and females starting at about age four... The hetero Establishment seems clueless that hetero boys will become hetero men regardless and that gay boys will become gay men despite all the propaganda and sports and shaming."—**Charles Nelson Reilly**

"The straight media and Establishment is selfish and petty. Just one gay role model horrifies them. One same-sex kiss threatens them. Even two men holding hands threatens them—but two men fighting, that's cool. The straights want it all, they don't want to share. Well, too bad. They no longer get all the say. Not unless we're passivist."—gay activist **Donna Red Wing**

"What they hate is when we're happy. It's one reason the status quo, like the *New York Times*, boycotts the word 'gay.' Instead, it's 'homosexuals'—sounds more clinical and less happy."—journalist **Lance Loud**

"What heterosexuals really fear is choice."
—bisexual **Andy Dick**

"Did you hear? Homosexuality has become legal in California. I'm getting out before it becomes compulsory."—comedian **Bob Hope**

"Did you hear the Statue of Liberty got AIDS? She got it from the Long Island Ferry."—**Bob Hope**, who later apologized for the "joke"

"It is nothing to sneer or laugh at, it is a horrible statement of fact. In the world today [2004], most of the nations where homosexuality remains a crime punishable by prison or death are Islamic or black—or both."—gay black actor **Roscoe Lee Brown**

"What I'm against is people who try to force a way of life or belief onto others—the missionary syndrome. That's what privately gave me pause about accepting the role of Eric Liddell. He was a Christian fanatic… but I accepted, for my career. If you look at *Chariots of Fire* [which won a Best Picture Oscar] it's quite anti-Jewish and it depicts Liddell as a near-saint. The movie is very effective propaganda that for a short time made me a star."—then-closeted British actor **Ian Charleson**

"Being closeted, and to a paranoid extent, meant Robert [Reed, *The Brady Bunch* father] avoided a committed relationship. Instead he cruised Pasadena in his car with dark-tinted windows and picked up tricks. No one special man, just anonymous frequent sex. Result: AIDS."—*Brady Bunch* creator-producer **Sherwood Schwartz** on the actor who died of AIDS

"I'm not sure why Tennessee Williams dumped Frank Merlo and I don't wish to speculate. They were a real couple. It was longer and had far more depth than an affair. I do know that after Frank died—of cancer, I believe—Tennessee regretted it for the rest of his life. He never found another truly devoted partner."—gay producer-writer **Dominick Dunne**

"I never met the great love of my life… I've wondered if it was my looks, my career or my being less shy around dogs. I always wanted someone who'd love me the way my dogs love me."—**Paul Lynde**

"It's a cautionary tale, sort of the curse of mainstream success. A young black singer who had a fun, loving relationship with another girl. Then comes fame and the closet and then a husband who's unreliable and at times abusive… The famous singer feigns happiness but becomes an addict… Was the fame and conformity worth it?"—music legal executive **Linda Wohl**

"Don't compromise your beloved, if you have one. One person you can love and be loved by all your life is more important than any temporary career advantage."—bisexual Oscar and two-time Tony winner **Sandy Dennis**

"The only abnormality is the incapacity to love."—writer-diarist **Anais Nin**

Chapter Four
Dishing in Public

Once a celebrity is known to be LGBT+, there's a variety of reactions from the public and media. Also from the gay community. Say a celeb comes out in middle age or later, some gays will say better late than never; others will say better never late, what took so long? Especially if said performer is retired.

Celebs have their own opinions about their peers, in or out. Today almost nobody is off-limits and little is considered too personal to touch on. While sometimes there's "too much information," the situation is healthier than in the days when showbiz figures had to change their names and stifle their opinions and individuality in order to seem like the majority of folks. What was too often deemed scandalous can now be disclosed without destroying a career. More and more, diversity and difference—not just how people look, but how they love—are acceptable.

"Only in America can a poor black boy like Michael Jackson grow up to become a rich white woman."
—comedian and Oscar-winning actor **Red Buttons**

"Lisa spends more time with her ex-husband Danny. This marriage is a total crock."—columnist **Sue Cameron** in 1995, on Michael Jackson and Lisa Marie Presley, who reportedly arrived and left in separate cars the night of Diane Sawyer's puff TV interview

"It's the most ridiculous thing I've ever known. Whenever I hear anything about that wedding I shut my ears because it upsets me so much. My boy [Elvis] would turn in his grave at the very thought of what Lisa Marie has gone and done. He'd be hurting bad."—**Colonel Tom Parker**, Elvis Presley's legendary manager

"In his teens Jackson had a blond boyfriend he fell in love with. Michael's father Joe crushed their relationship, he trampled it. Had Joe more power, it could have been worse. The lover of Frederick the Great of Prussia [northern Germany] was Hans von Katte, a handsome lieutenant. Before Frederick came to the throne his father had the man executed in front of his son, to end the relationship and 'toughen' him up."—openly bisexual Austrian actor **Helmut Berger** (*Ludwig*)

"Debbie Roe was an office assistant to Michael Jackson's plastic surgeon Dr. Steven Hoefflin. She agreed to marry Jackson and is the putative mother of the child Jackson claims is his... Wags are nicknaming the inevitable divorce proceedings *Roe versus Weird*."—*New York Daily News* cartoonist **Bill Gallo**

"The most normal man I know."
—**Elizabeth Taylor** on Michael Jackson

"After Michael Jackson became a solo singer he reached out to several older female stars... Kate Hepburn, Sophia Loren, Jane Fonda, Liz Taylor. When the molestation charges about the young boys surfaced and he started paying millions to quiet them, the ladies, even old friend Diana Ross, distanced themselves from him.

"The one who didn't was Elizabeth Taylor. She was more than ready to not be one of the bunch and to have him 'court' her with flattery, publicity and expensive gifts... His gifts continued... and she stayed loyal."—costume designer **Ray Aghayan**

"Elizabeth Taylor had a good heart but was over-fond of publicity, made several bad choices... After John Warner approached Barbara Walters, he latched on to Liz and she helped him win his Senate seat. She was a Democrat, semi feminist, pro-gay, but the Republican senator was in for 30 years, five six-year terms, consistently voting against women's rights and gay rights. Big boo-boo, Liz." —publicist **Andrea Jaffe**

"The first million-dollar check to fight AIDS was given by a Japanese philanthropist. The second by American magazine publisher Malcolm Forbes, who recruited Elizabeth Taylor to cloak his true sexuality.

"It was two converted Jewish women—Taylor and Dr. Mathilde Krim, wife of United Artists chief Arthur Krim—who helped start AmFAR, the American Foundation for AIDS Research. It went on to become the leading U.S. nonprofit dedicated to AIDS research and prevention."—**Richard Wherrett**, founding director of the Sydney Theatre Company (who died of AIDS)

146

"Elizabeth Taylor was turned down by several stars she invited to attend the first big AIDS fundraiser... Frank Sinatra said he didn't want to be involved with a 'fag disease.' The press was reporting AIDS as if it were a gay disease started by promiscuous male flight attendants. We now know it originated in Africa and that 70 percent of its victims, mostly in Third World nations, are heterosexuals."
—**Alexis Arquette** (*Last Exit to Brooklyn*)

"Even America's fashion industry hesitated to acknowledge or confront AIDS. Elizabeth Taylor wanted Calvin Klein to lend his support [to AmFAR's "To Care Is to Cure" fundraiser] but despite several requests he wouldn't. Klein, who was then in the closet, agreed to show up only after Dr. Mathilde Krim said Elizabeth Taylor would be his date if he helped."—European designer **Karl Lagerfeld**

"I remember Ray Sharkey's agent, after Sharkey died of AIDS, making sure that the media reported his death as caused by drug addiction and nothing but drug addiction... [hiding] the truth that Sharkey was bisexual, at least."—NBC staff photographer **Joey Del Valle**

"As Baby Jane would have said, 'But cha are, Lee, ya are!'"—fashion designer **Isaac Mizrahi** referencing Liberace's deathbed plea, "I don't want to be remembered as an old queen who died of AIDS."

"Show people are valued at a lower level than purely money people. Look at Jeffrey Epstein. Unlike most disgraced showbiz sexual abusers, straight or gay, as a level-three registered sex offender he remained socially acceptable, still mixing with VIPs in the arts, politics, film and finance.

"He socialized with the confident arrogance and sense of entitlement of a heterosexual male with endless wealth... Had Epstein been gay, all the money in the world wouldn't have gotten him all those coveted invitations."—investment banker **Ardavan Khodayari**

"If you don't think straight men own the media and shape the news, consider Epstein and [Harvey] Weinstein and other sex offenders trying to buy or actually buying periodicals specializing in reporting on celebrities... *Vanity Fair*, to name one periodical, censored damaging facts about Epstein, and the New York media generally turned a blind eye to his sexual activities. They sure wouldn't have done it for Kevin Spacey, who by the way once flew to Africa aboard Epstein's private jet."—Swedish blogger **Inger Nystrom**

"The stigma is doubled. There's already enough against homophile men as is, but then to die of AIDS... I understand the reluctance to admit it in an obituary. Still, it is a medical fact and most people who die of it are not gay men and many are not men."—gay actor **James Mitchell** (*All My Children*), who died at 89

"The average Anglo is more cold-blooded about it, they don't usually go into hysterics. Maybe from being used to less criticism. But if you're Latino, Hispanic, African American, the mere label of 'AIDS' tends to be the ultimate horror and shame."
—actor **Angel Lopez**

"There's a black basketball player, everyone knows his name… he was almost openly bisexual. Then he becomes HIV-positive, which to the media and man on the street—I guess there aren't women on the street—means 'AIDS,' although AIDS comes later. My point: once his diagnosis became known, you almost never again saw him without his wife by his side. Image wanted: heterosexual ex athlete."
—comedian **Yvette Tveidt**

"Some AIDS deaths are not admitted as such. Some people have the wealth to see to that, like Malcolm Forbes. Sometimes it's an intimidated press—in the U.S. jazz icon Miles Davis died of whatever, while in Europe AIDS was mentioned. Sometimes it's very pushy families withholding the cause of death altogether."—novelist **Jackie Collins**

"So many relatives of celebrities assume if they admit having a gay or bi relative the public will think the whole family's like that… Lorna Luft's memoir asserted that the only gay man in her whole family was half-sister Liza Minnelli's first husband Peter Allen, who died of AIDS. Never mind Judy Garland, Lorna's mother, being bisexual, or Judy's father Frank being kicked out of town in the Midwest ages and ages ago because of a scandal with a youth."
—biographer **C. David Heymann**

"Judy [Garland] and I were pals. It was always platonic between us… She had doubts about her own sexuality after she had an affair with a female singer [Kay Thompson]."—costar **Mickey Rooney**

Matrimonially: "Like mother, like daughter [Liza Minnelli]. A number of Judy Garland's husbands were gay. Vincente Minnelli certainly was."—jazz singer **Anita O'Day**

"Sweetie, he wasn't gay around me."
—**Dyan Cannon**, Cary Grant's fourth wife

"I knew he'd been married once and had a kid but he wasn't straight with me."—**David X**, lover and guest of closeted talk show host Merv Griffin

"We met when we were having an affair with the same man."—**Angela Bowie** on ex-husband David Bowie

"Some genders or nationalities are generally less objective. I'm cautious if I read a biography of someone I know or guess to be bi- or homosexual. For example [British poet] Stevie Smith. I read a bio of her by two American men. They denied she was bi. I also read a biography of her by an Englishwoman who admitted that Smith was bisexual. I should have known to skip the first book."—director **Anthony Harvey** (expectedly, the film *Stevie* starred Glenda Jackson as a straight Smith, with gay actor Alec McCowen as her boyfriend)

"I've read that Cary Grant and [actor] Randolph Scott were 'friends.' Or 'roommates.' They were far more than that... shared five separate houses, stayed in love for decades and kept in touch despite the marriages. Cary eventually had one kid, Randolph adopted. But they were each other's emotional mainstay. The wives came and went, they were professional and social necessities."—**Craig Zadan**, a producer of the Oscars telecast

"Here's how the press works. Cary Grant fathers his first and only child in his sixties. The press is ecstatic: jeez, what a man! The press doesn't question why Grant never had one in his twenties or his thirties, his forties or fifties. No, because it's all about hiding homosexuality and extolling heterosexuality."
—openly gay ICM agent **Ed Limato**

"Then these stars' kids come along, who know nothing of a gay parent's loves and relationships from before they were born—or even after—and some write books heatedly denying pop or daddy was gay. Plus these kids never know or use the more practical word 'bisexual.' These offspring aren't experts on their parents as anything but parents. They're not historians or film experts and they're often biased as hell."
—reviewer **Ginevra Becchio**

"The media used to be even worse… Tucker Smith deserved and got praise in the [film of] *West Side Story*. He was one of the Jets—acted, danced, dubbed the singing voice of the gang leader. It looked like Tucker was going places. One blind item [in a national column] about his private life ended it all. A *blind* item.

"Hollywood and its casting people shunned him… After he left the business he opened a bar called Tucker's Place north of Los Angeles, then died of AIDS."—**Leonard Bernstein**, who composed the music for *West Side Story*

"Tommy Tune [his real name] was a Broadway superstar who had small roles in two or three movie musicals. He was going to star in his own movie musical until a blind item got it wrong, said Tune had been seen in the audience of some New York show while wearing drag. The asshole who wrote the item confused the guy in drag with Tommy, who wasn't in drag. But that still cost Tommy his big movie debut."—**Steven Kolzak**, Senior V.P. of Talent & Casting at Columbia Pictures

"Why do we now negatively say that something 'sucks'? Because sucking is what gay men and women do... The language's insults are created to not put down heterosexuality or white men.... 'Straight' has several positive connotations... 'straight' people aren't necessarily straight. And it's the bigotry of the white male superstructure that 'sucks,' that is to say, that stinks."—philology professor **Robert Bourgault**

"It's finally come out how the studios arranged dates for gay stars and used us girls as decoys. I didn't mind going out with, say, Tab Hunter though I knew he'd end up with Tony Perkins, who was assigned his own female date. The four of us showed up in the limo, camera-ready, paraded into the cinema while smiling at the flashbulbs, then once inside, after the lights went out, Tab and Tony got up and went off together.

"The girl and I stayed and watched the movie. Nobody ever photographed anyone *leaving* a premiere."
—**Debbie Reynolds**

"As they say, like mother, like daughter. Debbie wasn't fond of men, hated all three husbands. You know she wanted to be a gym teacher? That's a stereotype, but... Carrie was *very* close to Penny Marshall. Carrie's daughter, you know, is by an openly gay talent agent who now has a husband. Carrie pretended she didn't know that, when they started going together—they never married. I think she just wanted to have the kid. That's what Debbie wanted too.

"For years now I keep hearing that Penny's very ill. But she's still here and Carrie's gone."—**Mary X**, lesbian friend of Debbie Reynolds and Carrie Fisher, in 2017

"I won't put it in my book... for the sake of the kids."—former singing star **Eddie Fisher**, after stating ex-wife Debbie Reynolds was "a lesbian" (her attorney threatened suit if his memoirs included the statement)

"In old Hollywood if you hired a publicist it was to get publicity. Today's Hollywood, if you're a big star and gay or lesbian, the publicist is to keep you deep in the closet."—gay actor **Craig Chester** (*Swoon*)

"I tried to kill myself because of all the anti-gay hate. I'm glad I survived, and I'm trying to make it better for the kids who come after me. To do this, and to express myself in my music, I had to be *me*, to come out. One can't create anything original or life-affirming from inside the closet."
—UK singer **Jimmy Somerville**

"Marcus Aurelius said a man's life is what his thoughts make of it. If, when you realize you're gay, you think it's terrible, then it is—for as long as you keep thinking that, and for no reason except that *they* who make the rules for all of us, who make themselves feel better by making us feel worse, *say* that it is.

"Are *they*, with their self-given rights and privileges, so much happier? Any better? They criticize us, make us an 'issue,' to distract from their own shortcomings and wrongdoings.

"Think for yourselves, brothers!"—**Dick Pabich**, who worked with Harvey Milk against California's Republican-sponsored Proposition 6, which would have banned gay teachers, and later against propositions that would have quarantined HIV-positive people

"I've found that life is about 20 percent what happens to us and 80 percent what our attitude is to that 20 percent... how we react to it and shape it, to our own advantage or to our disadvantage. So much of the choice is ours."—playwright **Lanford Wilson** (*The Fifth of July*)

"If they were actors I wouldn't confuse them. As a theatergoer I used to confuse the late playwrights Lanford Wilson and August Wilson. But not their work. Whatever Lanford's sexuality was, and I don't care, his plays include naturalistic gay characters. August's work is sexist and homophobic, as he was in his public comments." —**Bradford Dillman** (*Compulsion*)

"Judy Garland isn't the only actress who had more than one gay husband... It can be embarrassing when people get around to analyzing what draws non-heterosexual men to them. Such actresses often have an asexual or bisexual component that makes the bi or gay man feel more comfortable about marrying a woman."—film historian **Carlos Clarens**

"There's a Yank actress earnestly claiming that her entire past was heterosexual until *this* relationship. *Why* is she repeating this unlikely if not impossible declaration? Not for *her* sake, dears, for the sake of the men, including actors, with whom she was previously paired. Else, people might wonder about some of them—and well they should."—**Cilla Davies**, the "Welsh Tattler"

"I don't buy it. Anne Heche says she wasn't gay till she saw Ellen DeGeneres across a crowded room. Now, Ellen's an okay-looking chick, but not great-looking. Brad Pitt, *he's* great-looking. Still, I don't think if I saw him at a party I'd suddenly turn gay. Do you? Don't answer that!"—comedian **Rodney Dangerfield**

"The very first day [on *I Could Never Be Your Woman*] I had this scene where I was supposed to be making out with Michelle Pfeiffer. I told my wife, 'Look, I want you to know that I'm going to be making out with Michelle Pfeiffer today and I will be thinking about... Michelle Pfeiffer.' My wife's response was that when she makes out with me she also thinks of Michelle Pfeiffer."—**Paul Rudd**

"She did it on a dare... Julia is not gay."
—**Julia Roberts's publicist** in 1996 after the star was photographed dancing topless in a New York bar and kissing a female patron

"I have dated women."—**Sharon Stone**

"I'm dating women now. It's easier and more fun… also less stress. And you get to talk about yourself… you can discuss your feelings."—**Tatum O'Neal**

"Yes, of course it was platonic."—**Brooke Shields** on her arranged dates with Michael Jackson (Tatum O'Neal said the same thing)

"On his show, radio host Michelangelo Signorile brought up the rumors about Ron Reagan Jr. but also the rumors about his wife Daria… All too often, when a couple are both 'that way,' the rumors that see print are only about the male. The female is given more leeway—a sort of anti-gay gallantry."—writer and blogger **Murray Williams**

"I stopped listening to what Armistead [Maupin] told us about the closeted stars when he came in one morning and said that Paul Newman was gay!"
—**a female employee** at the *San Francisco Chronicle* (not gay, bi…)

"The homophobic movie critic Pauline Kael avowed that she couldn't believe in any role where Hollywood star Burt Lancaster enacted a bisexual, never mind gay. The silly cow lampooned his friendship and collaboration with [gay Italian director] Luchino Visconti. But Mr. Lancaster was bisexual, even if the facts didn't come out until he was gone."
—New Zealand critic **Trevor Collins**

"If a celebrity loves to get blown and his wife won't do it, or only twice a year, and he lets his male and sometimes female fans do it, does that make the man gay? No. Bisexual? I'm not sure. But why categorize? Why not just enjoy?"
—anonymous **talent manager** with "several such" male clients

"It boils down to 'is an individual pro-gay?' That's all we need to know. For instance I'd rather vote for a genuinely pro-gay heterosexual candidate than a gay Republican or any gay who's in the closet and only hears the sound of opportunity knocking. Fairness and integrity are what count, not who one canoodles with."—early gay rights activist **Harry Hay**, co-founder of the Mattachine Society, named after an Italian clown who wore disguises but always told the truth

"I don't believe that marriage. I think he's straight but likes being married to a celebrity though she's less of a star than during the series he produced. It's more evident why *she* married... after that female fan, as in fanatic, invaded her home and wanted to... whatever she wanted to do, but it turned out the fan was lesbian, so that was too close to home, *so...*"
—publicist **Ronnie Chasen**

"Some gays or bi's leave a gay partner when they want kids and prefer the other parent to be straight. That happened with Robert Taylor leaving Barbara Stanwyck for a German actress and it happened with Will Geer, who left gay rights activist Harry Hay. Of course nowadays anyone can have kids any old which way, and

157

why not?"—**Kenneth James Stump**, associate producer of *The Jeffersons* and *Good Times*

"The loyal viewership of that heart-warming TV series *The Waltons* would have had a collective seizure had it been widely known that Grandpa and Grandma Walton were queer in real life. Will Geer, who was blacklisted during the anti-communist witch hunts, had a male lover, and Ellen Corby had a relationship of several decades with her female companion. The women donated their large play collection to the West Hollywood library."—**Nancy**, a former WHPL librarian

"Honey, it's a scream how many TV series or movies got a gay actor in the cast… Look at *The Brady Bunch*—two or three—*Golden Girls, Will and Grace, The Jeffersons, Roseanne*… Look at *The Sound of Music*—one of the von Trapp kids and Uncle Max… "—**Nell Carter** (*Gimme a Break*)

"Watching *The Nanny*, I was more than surprised when the title character mentioned [NYC mayor] Ed Koch and England's Prince Edward as being gay. That's almost tangible progress. Past censorship would never have allowed that. It used to be considered an insult to say anyone was gay… also the fear of a lawsuit. But I don't think the royal family's allowed to sue—and they never have, have they?"—film and TV blogger **Sally Verdugo**

"This former male model became a TV star. He was publicly outed along with several other people—if I give details he might sue again. His alleged heterosexuality won him a settlement of five bucks. The 'undisclosed amount' wasn't made public and news reports made it sound like no, he is not gay, and those awful people who said he is had to pay dearly for smearing him. But settlement amounts leak out via the publisher or outfit that has to pay them—insiders know the amount, and sometimes tell."—entertainment journalist **Robin Leach**

"Then there's the small superstar who's a big nut case who every time he's described as gay sues for a humongous amount to scare them off. But there's so much that can be said about him, provably, so much evidence, with more coming out all the time... what I'm saying is, if he comes after me, he will truly regret the outpouring of truth...

"And if he or his people try anything, I have a mountain of info safely ready to go out to a dozen-plus news destinations upon my injury or death. That's how ruthless this control freak and those surrounding him are."—**anonymous author**

"Look, Molly, there's the man who killed all of Daddy's friends."—AIDS activist and former screenwriter **Larry Kramer** to his dog when Kramer bumped into his Manhattan neighbor Ed Koch

"Politicians almost can't sue. The public has the right to condemn their actions and personalities... their misdeeds and contradictions, e.g., lesbian Congresswoman Barbara Mikulski, who actually voted against gay marriage.

"Gay or lesbian politicians especially fear lawsuits and opening a can of worms... e.g., Ed Koch. For the longest time he avoided lifting a finger to combat AIDS... a liar, a hypocrite and a coward."—gay screenwriter **Arthur Laurents** (*The Way We Were*)

"I've heard two versions. When Koch became mayor he either gave up his boyfriend or he moved him to Washington [D.C.] to hide him away but keep him where he could visit him secretly with a professional pretext... I wonder if there'll ever be a movie about Ed Koch. Who could play him, now that Walter Matthau's gone?"—**former Congressional page** now working in Florida's capital, Tallahassee

"Body-building is psychologically complex and has more of a gay presence than one thinks. Pumping up all those muscles often compensates the man who feels less... Arnold Schwarzenegger was a crush of mine—until I saw his nude photo in *Spy* magazine. Building up the rest of the body made his already smallish you-know-what seem downright dinky. I got out my magnifying glass to be sure he was uncircumcised."
—impressionist **Charles Pierce**

"Schwarzenegger is a dummy and a hypocrite. He famously said he was okay with gay marriage as long as it was between a man and a woman. A hypocrite because as governor he vetoed gay marriage in California yet still said he was okay with it—and kept saying it after he tried to return to acting and into Hollywood's good graces. A total opportunist, and he almost made Reagan look smart."—**Donald Richie**, gay author and professor

"When he came on the scene I had a crush on Tom Brokaw the NBC news anchorman. But later... he's not at all pro-feminist, even less pro-gay... now writes books intended to be authoritative on American life that either marginalize or completely omit gay people... They say your attitude eventually shows on your face. I saw a recent photo of him—a sour, irritated expression."—documentary filmmaker **Rick McKay**

"A number of good-looking guys become more homophobic after getting hit on a lot of times. Their good looks, which society doesn't much prize that much, become an inconvenience or make them uncomfortable. I know it happened with Mel Gibson, from a conversation and a recent phoner with one of his ex [platonic] pals."—Australian writer **Gerald McGee**

"I don't know if gay men [rate] the face first, or the sexiness. Daniel Craig is not so handsome like a male model but I have to admit he is sexy. I enjoyed being the first bisexual James Bond villain [in *Skyfall*]... and to confront him in the flesh. It was fun. But more than that, I was able to shock much of my country [Spain], which has been traditionally so repressive... and I said in interviews that if I was gay I would marry a man just to tell the Church and what remains of its Inquisition to go to hell."—**Javier Bardem**

"I do want to play a gay James Bond... but time will tell if this project is possible in Hollywood. Where the straight James Bond has the Bond girls, you know, Ursula Andress or Graces Jones, I could, uh, rendezvous with Dennis Rodman, for instance."—**Rupert Everett** (the project didn't happen)

"Who's the bigot? That Mushnick guy [columnist] in *TV Guide* said I was bigoted for sounding off on the Mormons. What about how bigoted they are against blacks and gays and all? They go into states like Hawaii and Alaska and spend millions of dollars to kill the gay-marriage amendment things, you know."—athlete/actor **Dennis Rodman**

"It's so simple to retract a not exactly heterosexual image. Look at basketball player and actor Dennis Rodman. Some said he was moving toward coming out—gay or bi. Then he marries this *Baywatch* actress and most of the mainstream says, 'See, he was only fooling.'"—gay poet and translator **Paul Schmidt**

"Mick Jagger used to be almost openly bisexual. But as he ages, his image becomes all about womanizing... Aging isn't glamorous, so one means of retaining public appeal and interest is to opposite-sex-it. Young and single is one thing, middle-aged and single is suspicious and to some minds sad."—author **Carlos Clarens**

"I was amused by a British paper that said while the U.S. is more macho than France, France is more mature. It was about Richard Chamberlain coming out while in France and then his Hollywood publicist stoutly denying it and his agency persuading him to take it back. Richard did come out quite a bit later, after lead roles basically dried up and he was no longer 'king of the mini-series.'"—journalist **Lance Loud**

"I couldn't believe Bette Davis's comments on *The Thorn Birds* [TV mini-series]. First she says

Stanwyck was unbelievable in the role of a passionate older woman, then she also almost outs Richard Chamberlain as a lusty macho priest. Fortunately audiences didn't agree. But then, they weren't lusting after the role that Stanwyck got and that won her an Emmy."—*Thorn Birds* author **Colleen McCullough**

"Macho does not prove mucho. Ingrid Bergman told her ex-husband who told my masseuse she was friends with Cary Grant but he disliked doing the kissing scenes with her and other actresses. Me, I would have walked off the set. A man can at least *act* interested."—**Zsa Zsa Gabor**

"I liked that Michael Jackson shied away from playing it insensitive and macho. Until his head got swelled up he was appealing in an unusual way. He took the gender-less, race-less thing too far… but if I have to end this on a positive note I'll say at least he did not molest little girls."—singer **Nancy Wilson**

"The more there is macho, the more there is homophobia. It grows from insecurity. The insecure ones need to bully and dominate. In Latin countries a man must marry or be an outsider, always suspected. Even the funniest Mexican star, 'the Mexican Chaplin,' Cantinflas.

"We loved Cantinflas in Central America too. But he had to marry… even though an older woman. And have a son, even though adopted. People might not have believed any of it, but they wanted the images to reassure them."—gay Nicaraguan actor **Rene Enriquez** (*Hill Street Blues*)

"Eddie Murphy on *Saturday Night Live*... I thought he was funny and cute. Now he looks so hardened. I completely turned off him when he began doing those incredibly homophobic stand-up routines that went to DVD and are still in public libraries, where they should not be. If a comedian was verbally assaulting minorities other than gays there'd have been much less acceptance... Libraries are *public*, so let them know!"—**X**, a Beverly Hills Public Library reference librarian

"I feel sorrier for the black gay kids... it's more of a taboo than with the whites. I've read and I've heard mamas say they rather have a son in jail than a son that's a homosexual... So when you hear some black comic ripping gays apart it's really his way of saying he's not gay. Not that it excuses that, but you understand?"—**Charles Murphy** (Eddie Murphy's brother)

"When Mel Gibson debuted on the U.S. scene the press called him Australian although he wasn't born there. Down Under they'll tell you he's American. His dad, a Holocaust denier, took the brood to Australia in the 1960s when the U.S. was getting 'too liberal,' also he didn't want his myriad sons going to fight in Vietnam, which you'd think being so far-right he'd be all for that war."—**Barb Taylor**, U.S. free-lancer for the Sydney-based magazine *Lesbians on the Loose*

"In Mel Gibson's very first movie he kisses another guy on the lips. It's been alleged that the scene was spontaneous. Regardless, Gibson loathes the picture, always calls it 'an abomination.' How biblical."—gay comedian **Bob Smith**

"Don't trust Hollywood for history. They twist facts totally... Parliament was in a tizz when a recent World War II film changed the nationality of the anti-Nazi heroes from British to American. Or... Mel Gibson's insertion of anti-gay violence that was played for laughs into his *Braveheart* fantasy that won him a Best Director Oscar. Shameful. Shameful [AMPAS] *voters*."
—**Jimmy Somerville** (the film also won Best Picture)

"Paul Newman is box office but that means nothing when his intended next project is gay-themed. On top of that, it's set in the sports world, so almighty sacred to straight men, and it's a love story between a coach and an athlete. Hollywood wouldn't touch it... Mr. Newman approached Robert Redford, with whom he made two enormous hits. Redford turned him down, didn't want to play gay."—**Jerry Wheeler**, would-be producer of a film of the novel *The Front Runner*, a gay love story

"Such anti-Establishment news leaks out very slowly. Paul Newman did go both ways. Big deal. But to the powers that be, it is a big deal when a male superstar isn't what he's 'supposed' to be, to keep all the boys from 'becoming' gay. I commend Paul for trying to make a movie of my novel. He tried hard but a brick wall is hard too."—novelist **Patricia Nell Warren**, who also wrote a novel, *The Beauty Queen*, inspired by homophobe Anita Bryant

"One of the all-time male heartthrobs was buried with a topless photo of his male lover in his shirt's right pocket, apart from the public wedding band on his left hand. I saw this for myself at an L.A. mortuary, as funeral homes were called, where my older boyfriend worked. I hadn't decided whether to join the business… he invited me there one night to discuss my future and for 'a special surprise.'

"I assumed the surprise would be sexual, but it was… *him*. I'd been a huge fan and to see him there, inside a casket and touchable—I almost fainted when I very carefully touched his face. Only. And I wouldn't have believed about the photo, but I *saw* it, with *his* name handwritten on the back… I finally chose this business because I couldn't get a teaching job. Still, no regrets."
—anonymous **San Francisco funeral home director**

"The Burt Reynolds estate auction [in June 2019] has nothing to do with me, but reading about it reminded me of something I've never read about, so feel free to use it… Say a movie star is secretly gay or he's AC/DC, like Reynolds. When he dies, an associate or relative, say, goes through his belongings and before any auction—before official sorting or appraisal, before anything that can reach the media—the star's 'give-away' items are shunted to one side.

"Those could be anything from the guy's dildo or other sex toys, his collection of old *Playgirl* or *Viva* magazines, personal photos, love-type letters, porn tapes and DVDs, homoerotic statues and artworks, you name it.

"A relative will likely burn, shred or otherwise trash those items. An associate, a trusted employee—

or also even a gay relative—or auctioneer might keep some, then, very quietly and unofficially, sell the 'give-away' items to interested but discreet parties—often very closeted non-famous men with money to spare… Those unofficial items can fetch better prices than the official stuff."
—retired **Los Angeles auctioneer Howard E.**

"The Establishment no longer rewards racists. But homophobes still get a pass. A Mel Gibson wasn't censured for anti-gay comments or depictions in his movies. Not till he went all-out anti-Jewish did he fall out of favor, and even that temporarily… It's up to gays to protest the homophobes and their words and actions and the rewards they get for them. And boycott their movies."—**Taylor Negron** (*The Last Boy Scout*)

"I am a proud member of P-FLAG, Parents and Friends of Lesbians And Gays, a national organization. I love and support my gay daughter… anyone who doesn't love their gay child is not a true parent."
—Ellen's mother **Betty DeGeneres**

"It's a fairly small minority compared to the whole. So we must enlist the backing and acknowledgment of our families… and what family doesn't have a GLBT member, even if not in the immediate family? *All* of us need to stand up to homophobia —in politics, religion, entertainment or elsewhere."—five-time Grammy-winning singer/songwriter **Amy Winehouse**

"My relatives came around to accepting my difference. But they still won't tell anyone outside the family circle. They won't say so, but they're still ashamed. Which is idiotic—I'm not!"—**John Megna**, who played Dill, friend of the children of Atticus (Gregory Peck) in *To Kill a Mockingbird*

"In my country a woman must by law cover her head or be punished in the name of male-designed religion. I cannot expect support for my freedom from my father or brothers. I have to turn to my mother and aunts and sisters, but there is too little support there— there is too much fear, too little unity."—anonymous **gay Iranian actress** living in France

"Men are larger, so they have scared and dominated women from the start... they punish women and give themselves immunity. As with adultery. It used to be instant grounds for divorce if a wife cheated. But not necessarily if a man cheated. And among Muslims, in some countries still, an adulteress can be stoned to death. While the men can cheat to their non-existent hearts' content."—UK-based Egyptian feminist lecturer **Amina Said**

"Men are afraid women will laugh at them. Women are afraid men will kill them... not an entirely unfounded fear. Most murdered women are killed by husbands or boyfriends, or ex-husbands or ex boyfriends."—**Carrie Fisher**

"It isn't that I hadn't ever considered [a lesbian relationship]. I'd say, 'Well, would that be interesting? Would I want to?' And I honestly don't think that the thought ever resolved itself."—**Julie Andrews**

"One of the more famous bits of showbiz gossip is that Carol Burnett and Julie Andrews were at a hotel while taping one of their joint TV specials. One day, out in the hall, as a joke, they pretended they were kissing. Who at that moment should appear but Mike Nichols, a closet case and a gossip who spread the story far and wide? Poor Carol and Julie had to 'explain' about it for years after."—columnist **Richard Gully**

"If I ever had any doubts [about being gay] they stopped when I got the record album of *The Sound of Music* and spent hours staring at the back-cover photo of Julie Andrews, so beautiful with that smile and short hair and eyes and freckles and... I loved it!"—award-winning stage actress **Cherry Jones**

"I have too much respect for men [to marry them]. Another reason I'm not very inclined toward marriage is that it ends too many friendships, and I value friendship highly—my friendships with ladies and with gentlemen. And *all* of my men friends are gentlemen."—silent and talkies star **Lillian Gish**, revealing perhaps more than she intended about her private life

"There are some lesbians who will admit to being bi—only—because of their ex-husbands. Otherwise people will wonder if the guy was gay, and often a lesbian's ex-husband is."—columnist **Lee Graham**

"While in Los Angeles I was channel-surfing and paused on one of those ghastly evangelist shows. The junior evangelist, lamely following in his father's super-rich footsteps, was shouting that masturbation is 'a homosexual deed!' Here's why: when a man plays with himself he's handling a penis! In that case, most of the world's men are homosexual, indeed!"—UK actor **Michael Sheen** (*The Queen, Frost/Nixon*)

"Wouldn't it be wonderful if the only way you could get AIDS was by contributing money to television evangelists?"—comedian **Elayne Boosler**

"Those anti-gay people say homosexuality can't be 'natural' because animals don't do it. But they're lying. Animals *do* it. Only, they don't do it in the documentaries we grew up with from Disney or the ones on TV even now."—actress **Morgan Fairchild**, who trained to be an anthropologist

"… Actors were sometimes surprised by the on-camera behavior of the animals [in Tarzan movies]. Especially the chimp, which was a large male, passionately in love with Johnny Weissmuller. Whenever he came on the set the chimp not only sat on his haunches and howled with delight, he also showed unmistakable signs of his homosexual affection and you couldn't shoot on him until his ardor cooled off.

"'Okay,' the director would sigh, 'lights out. Everybody sit down and wait, please.'"
—actress **Lilli Palmer** in her memoir *Change Lobsters and Dance*

"After Pee-Wee Herman [Paul Reubens] was arrested while playing with himself in that porn theatre

what the media did not admit was it was his second arrest there in Sarasota, where his parents lived. Most of the media didn't admit that. None of the media admitted Reubens is gay."
—screenwriter **Arthur Laurents** (*The Turning Point*)

"The place where [Paul Reubens] was arrested was showing heterosexual porn. He didn't go for what was on the screen, he went for the horny male audience. Luckily for him, that town didn't have a gay adult theatre..."—costume designer **Scaasi** (Arnold Isaacs; the last name is Scaasi, backwards)

"If you're gay and saw *Hello, Dolly* with Barbra Streisand you certainly noticed Danny Lockin, the charming 5'6" hunk who played Barnaby Tucker... He married and had a kid but later came out... At 34 in a gay bar in Garden Grove, California, he met a gay sadist who'd been in the Air Force. Danny went home with him and was later found in the man's apartment, stabbed over 100 times. The murderer got about four years' prison time. You know why? Basically because he only killed a gay man... After the killer got out he lived a quarter century longer."—gay archivist **Jim Kepner**

"Who says Joan of Arc wasn't lesbian? Although she led a French army and defeated the English occupiers of France, the French branch of the Church burned her at the stake. For them her unpardonable sin was her insistence on wearing men's clothes. They said it went against their male god... Centuries later, because people still revered Joan's memory, the Church traded on her popularity by officially making her a saint. Fat lot of good it did her."—women's studies professor **Irma Lederer**

"Back when germs were far more deadly than today there was Typhoid Mary, a cook blithely spreading disease. Early in the 20th century she was caught... by a then-rare female doctor who happened to be a lesbian."—**Marya Odalapo**, N.P.

"The history scandal is twofold. That so many gay and lesbian historical figures are deliberately mislabeled as heterosexual and that so many were so awfully mistreated unless they were rulers. Even some gay rulers had it horribly bad—I can think of one English king, a Prussian emperor and a Turkish sultan, to name just three."—UCSB professor **Philip "Felipe" Powell**

"Practically nobody knows that the first actress to win an Academy Award was gay—Janet Gaynor. Or that the first four were all Canadian—her and Mary Pickford and Norma Shearer and Marie Dressler, who was gay too. No one in the U.S. knows those four were Canadian. We've produced so many great people, but then they go south and get swallowed up in an American identity.

"About the only famous Canadians to Americans are k.d. lang, who's gay, and me. And half of them haven't heard of me, which is *scandalous*!"
—**Scott Thompson** of the Kids in the Hall

"... A faggoty dress-up party."—Canadian Supreme Court Justice **Ian Binnie** at a Phi Delta Phi initiation banquet in Toronto commenting on fraternity rituals; after the adjective caused an uproar he apologized, rejecting the word and "the pejorative attitude that lies behind it"

"Sometimes they try to fag me up and I have to put my foot down. [My character] has all these fruity little traits that come out every week, and they try to whiz them past me… [When] I get too faggy, they have me make out with a chick."—**David Spade**, criticizing his *Just Shoot Me* producers in *Playboy*; after GLAAD (the Gay & Lesbian Alliance Against Defamation) criticized his comments, Spade explained via his spokesman that the comments were just "good-natured;" GLAAD declined the lame semi apology

"I always feel when somebody calls you a star it's like they're saying 'fag.'… When somebody says 'star' I hear 'pussy.' I don't know why."—actor **David Duchovny** in *Esquire* magazine; GLAAD criticized his "juvenile remarks," prompting Duchovny to say he'd always supported his gay friends and wished he'd used a different negative word (presumably not the f-word)

"Being a star is tough, it brings its own set of problems one hadn't imagined. Being a gay star—whether in or out—is even tougher. Apart from anything else, it attracts more spite and envy, more blind hate, more risks to your career, more supposed scandals because you're not typical, whatever typical is… You really must give openly gay actors credit for their extreme courage and optimism."—openly gay British actor **Alec McCowen** (*Travels with My Aunt*)

"My wife Gracie [Allen] loved scandal. I didn't. Those things didn't interest me. I'm not interested in anything that happened yesterday. And how can you deal with Cary Grant's homosexuality?"—actor and author **George Burns**

"Gossip is fun, but only if it's true. The columns and celebrity rags make up heteromances for closeted stars. That's not fun, it's phony—manufactured for financial reasons. Also, it gives a bigoted impression if you can read between the lines."—**Nancy Kulp** (*The Beverly Hillbillies*)

"Roslyn Kind is a wonderful singer and nice person, but she's better known as Barbra Streisand's kid half-sister. Roz's husband Randy Stone was a gay man who died prematurely but not from AIDS. Did Roz know? Why did she marry him? What does Barbra think? Babs's only child is an openly gay man. Rather fascinating!"—comedian **Shelley Berman**

"Jodie Foster was up for a third Academy Award, so her publicity machine put it out that she'd found the man of her dreams and he'd moved in with her. Most columnists bought it. My colleague Arlene Walsh pooh-poohed it, and I didn't even mention it. Soon after Ms. Foster didn't win, her non-beau [producer Randy Stone] came out of the closet. Greed and duplicity..."—*Beverly Hills (213)* columnist **Richard Gully**

"Jodie Foster looked so uncomfortable when she did male-and-female love scenes... she did fewer and fewer as time went on... I used to wonder why she took so long to come out, as she wasn't a sex symbol or pin-up. But she did, and now she prefers to direct. Good for her."—**Patty Duke**, also an Oscar winner and former child star

"There was one Charlie's Angel who refused to do cheesecake and pin-up shots. Guess why. But she never came out and is now reportedly almost a recluse."—photographer **Rick Coffman**

"Kate Hepburn was one of very few newcomers then who wouldn't pose in swimsuits, have her hair dyed blonde, etc. It's a wonder the studio [RKO] didn't let her go, because they were scandalized that she never wore a skirt except in character. Eventually she publicly teamed with Spencer Tracy, a bisexual. They covered each other… but they did become best friends."—*Hollywood Reporter* editor **Frank Barron**

"Somebody told me that a famous, sexy blonde American actress had a crush on me. I wasn't surprised when I learned the name, and I'm flattered. It only surprises me she isn't in the open about bisexuality, as her image and screen roles have been *very* sexual."—**Isabella Rossellini**

"An actress who admits that she finds other women appealing or has had a same-sex affair may actually expand her fan base."—**Neil Patrick Harris**

"She's had very bad luck with men, so why not move a female lover into Kensington Palace? Di would have lipstick lesbians lining up to woo her, and adding a —ke to her name would have maximum tabloid effect."—novelist **Jackie Collins** to the Australian press about Princess Diana

"If Caitlin Jenner is truthfully attracted to women, does he or she admit to now being lesbian? Or is she not a lesbian?"—"king of the paparazzi" **E.L. Woody**

"I didn't know that the vast majority of male-to-female transsexuals haven't had The Operation. They've taken hormones, they've gotten breasts, but they haven't gotten rid of *it*. So obviously they're not women, though they dress and make up as women. It's closer to being a drag queen. Sorry, but that's the truth."—photographer **Herb Ritts**

"Some tomboys remain tomboys—a fact some parents have to face. One can't know ahead of time. You can only support your child lovingly, whoever they are."—bisexual actor **Brad Davis** (*Midnight Express*), whose daughter Alexandra became a male

"Warren Beatty's daughter becomes a... his son. If the parents can deal with it, why can't the culture? It's not the country's business and it's not threatening, unless one's too easily threatened."—**Carrie Fisher**

"One tabloid ascribed Chastity Bono's decision to become a man to her mother [Cher] having admitted to a few affairs with women in her youth. As if parents can influence their kids' sexuality! If that were so, there'd be virtually no gay people. All parents can do is induce guilt. Preferably not."—New York casting director **Bernie Styles**

"Tabloids on both sides of the Atlantic are ignorant and arch-conservative, which is redundant. I couldn't believe it when several tabloids blamed O.J. Simpson's being a wife-batterer and alleged double-murderer on the fact that his father was a cross-dresser. Read their stupid headlines if you must, but boycott those rags!"—**George Michael**

"I don't put down Cher's ex daughter Chastity, now Chaz. But she or he claims not to be a lesbian because of feeling 'like a man.' So did Margaret Thatcher. And I recall how Cher's child put down Ellen DeGeneres's TV show after Ellen came out for being 'too gay.' Has anyone ever put down a TV show for being 'too straight'?"—UK actor **Alec McCowen**

"I think because of my masculinity I would [costar] with somebody very feminine, like Michelle Pfeiffer. Actually, I find Michelle Pfeiffer fantastically attractive. I'm always kind of rushing up to her and kissing her on the mouth because she's so delicious. She's so-o-o delicious."—two-time British Oscar winner **Emma Thompson** (for acting and writing)

"Men need liberating more than women do. Top actresses today can be very sexually frank. Only male comedians and supporting actors can be somewhat frank. Top actors still live in a gilded cage. If they admit to just one gay fantasy or a long-ago crush, never mind an actual affair, it's curtains."
—**Anne Jeffreys** (*General Hospital*)

"If a man or woman compliments a woman's looks, she is pleased. If a man compliments a man's

177

looks, the recipient, if he isn't homosexual, may feel confused, suspicious or angry. Even violent. Male culture is too volatile."—gay actor **Elliott Reid** (*Gentlemen Prefer Blondes*)

"If a man finds [another man] attractive, the other man may erupt in anger and violence. I witnessed this at a Hollywood party attended by a married Scientologist movie star who's known for coming onto male caterers. The police were almost summoned and money had to change hands."—author Dr. **Betty Berzon**

"Being an actor is educational about a broad range of people. Like, several guys have come on to me, and if I wasn't an actor... but you get to see it's harmless. I just say no or thanks anyway... If I wasn't an actor I'd never have been inside of a gay bar. That really showed me how 'everyday' gay guys are." —**Luke Perry** (*Beverly Hills 90210*)

"Very, very pretty in a Gothic-painting sort of way."—**Neil Patrick Harris** on actor Johnathon (sic) Schaech

"Excellent actor, very attractive, very charismatic. I don't mind losing parts to Matt."—**Harris** on Matt Damon

"Men, period, know very little about lesbians. One proof is that when we learn some gorgeous guy is gay we're not surprised. But if a gorgeous woman turns out to be a lesbian we're often surprised—*she's* lesbian? I wonder why that is."—gay attorney **Tom Stoddard**

"I'm very deadpan and I'm bald. People are sometimes surprised to learn I'm gay. Or they're dismayed. I'm not the positive stereotype, the handsome sexy youth. That's a minority within a minority."
—**Richard Deacon** (*The Dick Van Dyke Show*)

"It's easier for handsome actors to get hired, so long as they're not obvious or too open. If you're not handsome it's harder to get hired but you may get more worthwhile parts. You won't become a star but you won't lose the great looks you never had. Still, unless you plan to do lots of stage work, you'll probably need a regular job outside showbiz."
—**John Megna** (*The Cannonball Run*)

"The process of directing or acting is wonderful but should be private. It's the result that matters to the spectator. Don't bore us with the process. In other words, I do not mind seeing the artist naked, but I hate to see him undressing. Show me your cock. That's all right with me. But don't striptease."
—actor-director **Orson Welles**

"In school I had an acquaintance—straight and very condescending—who was so good-looking that he boasted he was going to Hollywood. To do what? I asked facetiously. 'To be a star, dummy!' He did go, returned half a year later, then went back when he got an offer from an agribusiness company near L.A. But as the song says, I'm still here..."—**Leonard Frey** (*The Boys in the Band*)

"I look forward [in 2018] to the stage revival of *The Boys in the Band*. We've yet far to go, but how far

179

we've come! Some 50 years back, its gay cast members stayed put in the closet... merely appearing in a gay-themed play stigmatized all the cast.

"All of the revival's cast members are openly gay—the director is too—and successful. Our community, with hardly anyone else's help, has forced this change."—**David Ogden Stiers** (*M*A*S*H*)

"Self-representation is the key reason the U.S. Colonies became independent of Britain. Yet for centuries gay men have permitted straight men to misrepresent us in every medium... in books and later in movies. Gay men have been lied about so often and so perniciously that even today the average person still believes most of those lies. Only we can change that—and we've finally begun. We need to become independent of the heteros."—writer **Paul Monette**

"Truth to tell, if it were up to only straight men, powerhouse women like Bette Davis and Barbra Streisand would not have become stars. They weren't 'fuck-able' enough for straight men... Gay men in the arts can discern and appreciate talent and individuality in a given female. Straight men are usually just ogling her and assessing their chances."—**Christopher Isherwood**

"What too many gay men don't realize is they must be allies with not only lesbians but women in general. Every country, society and religion which discriminates against women discriminates against gay men. The two bigotries go hand in glove. Like it or not, traditionalists have always associated gays with women. You can't have gay rights unless you have women's rights."—journalist-author **Oriana Fallaci**, who defiantly removed her head-covering while interviewing the Ayatollah Khomeini

"A bigoted business executive once asked Harvey Milk what on earth gays and lesbians have in common, since gays like men and lesbians like women? Harvey's answer: 'We have you in common.' The bigot doesn't differentiate; he just sees people who love their own kind, and he hates that."—journalist and ex actor **Dale Reynolds**

"The Equal Rights Amendment was and is needed [because] women are not in the Constitution. If they were, it wouldn't have required a special amendment to give women the vote."—**Carol Burnett**, mother of an openly bisexual daughter

"Our slogan is 'liberty and justice for all.' Right. Yet something as fair and simple as the Equal Rights Amendment was defeated. The Right, including right-wing women, jumped on it and totally misrepresented it, and the media played 'neutral' and went along with them. 'Neutral.' Right. Like Switzerland with the Nazis."—**Alex Comfort**, author of *The Joy of Sex*

"Too many gay men and lesbians—in fact too many women, period—retain some degree of internalized bigotry... of self-hate... from the propaganda everyone grew up with."—Dr. **Ruth Westheimer**, whose family perished in the Holocaust

"No one can make you feel inferior without your consent."
—apparently bisexual First Lady **Eleanor Roosevelt**

"You do realize nearly all lesbian-themed films were directed by men, and most still are. What has to change is valuing women solely for their looks. Look what that did to Marilyn Monroe... The entire social structure must change, so it's not just or even mostly men who get to evaluate."—**Emma Thompson**

"I'm not gay but we were working together and when John [Travolta] flirted with me I was flattered... 'cause of his looks then and who he was. When a star flirts you're always flattered. Unless maybe you're a star too."—**Jeff Conaway** (*Grease*)

"Oprah knew he was gay but when Barry Manilow was on her show she asked what kind of woman he preferred... A friend told me about an X-rated movie titled *The Private Life of Brandon Manilow*... with an Eastern European porn star named Brandon Manilow. I wonder how Barry feels about that? Flattered or furious?"—gay playwright **Edward Albee**, winner of three Pulitzer Prizes

"It's okay if Donna Summer or Anita Bryant or Gloria Gaynor dislike homosexuals and say so, but if someone says he dislikes 'born-again' Christian singers, black or white, that's not okay, somehow. The message is it's okay to put down some minority groups but not others. Yet music is supposed to be the universal language of love.

"If you want the truth, and I can say this, singers tend to be even dumber than actors, and more bigoted."—singer-activist **Michael Callen**

"The late Whitney Houston would never have come out, so I couldn't be discussing probably the most hushed-up movie scandal of the 1980s. It was during shooting of *The Accused*, which won Jodie Foster an Oscar. She and costar Kelly McGillis of *Top Gun*, the Tom Cruise film, were having an affair. Kelly was allegedly also having one with Whitney.

"Jodie apparently either found them or found out and allegedly punched Kelly in the jaw. Shooting had to shut down for a week or more. McGillis later retreated from acting and came out; Foster came out after about 50 years in the business. But not Whitney."—**Linda Wohl**, music legal executive at Paramount for three decades

"It's not often a star walks away from Hollywood. Kristy McNichol did... after two TV series, several movies and much praise. I believe she's now a hairdresser. Kristy came out [in 2012] to support young lesbians and gays [since] 30 percent or more of teen suicides are owed to homophobia. Bravo Kristy!"—TV star **Meredith Baxter** (*Family Ties*), who came out in 2009 and played Kristy's older sister in *Family*

"Jaye Davidson was a [gay] nominee for Best Supporting Actor for *The Crying Game*. His was one of the first penises seen in a mainstream movie—it had to be, to prove that the straight guy in love with him was in love with a male. Jaye works as a fashion assistant in London. Do you know what he said at the time? I looked it up:

"'Oh, no, I hope I don't win the Oscar. I'm not an actor, and if I won it wouldn't be fair to the other people who are actors.' That is *so* un-Hollywood."—gay or bi actor **Dom DeLuise**

"The media correctly denounced John Lennon's assassin but never breathed a word how stupid the guy was. He had a 'love obsession' with Jodie Foster and thought by killing a major celebrity he could impress and win her. Boy, did he have a wrong number."—gay or bi producer **Daniel Melnick** (*Making Love*)

"The show business code says a leading lady doesn't snitch on the gay male costar she's made love with onscreen. But Cary Grant wasn't a very nice fellow and made numerous enemies who didn't admit it because Grant was so overrated and admired. The business was in awe of the fact that at 65 he actually retired. Most men stars keep acting and making money till they shrivel up or drop.

"However picturesque a couple Grant and my wife made on screen, it was all make-believe. The man was as queer as a two-dollar bill. I shouldn't say that, I'm not intolerant. Just say he was gay. The whole industry knew—but didn't tell."

—TV director **Jeffrey Hayden**, whose wife Eva Marie Saint costarred with Grant in Hitchcock's *North by Northwest*

"Be careful who you flatter. Like if you once had a crush on a handsome movie star, then years later you

get to meet him and he's let's say not so handsome but you compliment him anyway, to be nice. I did, and Tony Curtis replied, 'Wanna go down on me?'"
—**Ron Vawter** (*Philadelphia*)

"In Hollywood the most common one-on-one sex act is a blow job. Most straight guys will take one off a gay or bi guy, and agents are so spoiled... a female starlet told one agent if he'd consider her for a certain role she'd fellate him. The agent replied, 'Yeah, but what's in it for me?'"
—Canadian playwright **John Herbert** (*Fortune and Men's Eyes*)

"It was fun playing Liberace but the movie couldn't include all his wit and one-liners... like 'What's better than roses on your piano? Tulips on your organ.' As a formerly promiscuous heterosexual I could relate to his being promiscuous in his own way."—**Michael Douglas**

"I've had my cock sucked by five of the big names in Hollywood."—**James Dean**

"Once at a [talk show] taping in front of a sizeable audience Eva Gabor was there. So was a well-known closeted gay man [who] came on wearing a very summery seersucker suit—he looked great in it. So Eva, in one of those whispers that half the audience can hear, said to him, 'Dahling, I adore your cocksucker suit!'"
—author **Paul Rosenfield** (*The Club Rules*)

"Many people were shocked to find out Nancy Reagan's godmother was Russian and a lesbian—Alla Nazimova, a highly-paid actress and producer, almost forgotten. Those people would be more shocked to read in a biography by one of Peter Lawford's wives that pre-Reagan, Nancy Davis had actor dates whom she favored with an act I will not name."—author **Richard Condon**

"The average squirrel can keep nuts in his mouth for months on end, and everyone's impressed. And yet when poor Clay Aiken does it, everyone's nauseous." —**Joan Rivers** in her book *Diary of a Mad Diva*

"The ignorance about gays and music... How many people know a gay man wrote 'I Left My Heart in San Francisco'? Or that 'The Wind Beneath My Wings' was written by a man to a man? You don't find this in popular music books."—singer **Lesley Gore** ("You Don't Own Me")

"Kathy Bates the actress says marriage is definitely not for her. *Brava*. But what male star will say that? He'd then have to explain himself, he couldn't just leave it at that."—**Julie Harris** (*East of Eden*)

"You know Prince is part white and he's pretty and he's successful and that's why Michael Jackson has a crush on him but hates him. I'm not making this up. Mention Prince to Michael and then watch his retooled face try and contort and react."—gay black writer **E. Lynn Harris**

"Stephen Sondheim is admirable as a composer-lyricist. Less so as a gay man who sometimes wrote anti-gay lyrics and reportedly didn't come out until after his mommy died."—music critic **Pietro Cavaluzzi**

"There's an English movie actor, first name Michael... played bi and gay more than once. Now past his commercial prime yet still enmeshed in matriphony—no kids involved. Whether the older woman is also gay, I don't know. If he sues over this, we can find out a whole lot of things."—Monty Python member **Graham Chapman**

"The English aren't so awed by their talented actors. Americans are over-awed and overrate them. Like Laurence Olivier... such a god to the Yanks that they won't come near to revealing that he's basically gay, tremendously ambitious and selfish... and rotten to gay actors like John Gielgud who don't choose to hide behind wives and tots."—Australian biographer **Charles Higham**

"Larry [Olivier] used to be beautiful—too physically beautiful for Hollywood. I once caught him in his dressing room after a stage performance, staring at himself in the mirror. His expression told all: he was in love. After he got over his embarrassment he told me he was so enthralled by his own image that his biggest regret in life was not being able to go down on himself."—**Orson Welles**

"American press reportage often leaves big gaps... Decades ago, *Time* reported that John Travolta

187

wanted to leave Scientology but was allegedly blackmailed to stay. Decades after, *People* or some such magazine reported that during a Caribbean vacation two locals, a husband and wife, tried to blackmail Travolta but were arrested. The reportage in both cases did not include: blackmailed about *what*?"—French journalist **Yves Bouchard**

"Money-made or fear-based marriages often outlast straight ones, which on the husband's part are often based on lust. Very few straight Hollywood marriages stay the course."—**Sandra Bullock**

"Some people are bigger than their incomes. Most movie stars are not."—**Victor Buono** (*What Ever Happened to Baby Jane?*)

"Everybody wants to be Cary Grant. I want to be Cary Grant."—**Cary Grant**

"Your identity and sense of security should go beyond what you do for money. One of my favorite quotes is from Cervantes, author of *Don Quixote*: '... she feared wagging tongues, and when I asked her to describe her soul, she detailed her wardrobe.'"
—**Michelle Rodriguez** (*Furious Seven*)

"They can cancel my show, but they can't cancel me."—**Ellen DeGeneres**

"There's a group of older people out there that will never accept [homosexuality], but there are a lot of empty cemeteries, and when they're filled, the world will be more tolerant."—**Tim Doyle**, openly gay executive producer and head writer of *Ellen*, shortly after the sitcom's cancellation in 2002

"It's only a gilded cage."—closeted gay or bisexual movie star **Tyrone Power** on a star's life

"To not admit I'm gay would be to live my life like a 24-hour spy or a caged animal, watching my every move, every word, any indication of who I really am, afraid that everyone's staring at me, judging, ready to pounce or shoot."—Canadian playwright **John Herbert**

"When you have these insane armed fanatics and haters who go out and shoot down gays or Jews, it always strikes me that two can play that game… in other words, shoot back!"
—lesbian activist **Donna Red Wing**

"In the 21st century of this particular calendar, Brunei and its sultan are still living in a barbaric Dark Ages that no civilized people should put up with. As with apartheid in South Africa decades ago, this should be an international human rights issue and a subject of immediate boycott."—**Katherine Helmond** (*Who's the Boss?*) in 2008, referring to the Islamic country's draconian punishments for same-sex activity and adultery; in 2019 its sultan decreed the death penalty for gay sex

"The law to stone their citizens is still in place. Meaning that as soon as the pressure dies down they could simply start the process of carrying out executions."—**George Clooney** in 2019 after Brunei backed off on killing gay men due to pressure from corporations and banks (the sultan owns the Beverly Hills and Bel-Air hotels in Los Angeles, also London's Dorchester, the Plaza Athénée in Paris, etc.)

"The response to Brunei, also to Indonesia, Malaysia and other Muslim lands enacting medieval laws has not been that strong… indicating that even in the 'modern' world gay lives are not of major concern to most people."—Japanese journalist **Keiko Komiyama**

"It's this basic. The worst thing a gay man of today can do is live in the closet, hide his core self from relatives, friends, coworkers, everyone, plus hide behind a woman. Unless that man has no romantic feelings and no sex drive whatever, he is less than worthless—the lowest kind of liar and a betrayer to himself, his kind and the future."—**Scott Forbes**, gay activist and managing partner of West Hollywood's Studio One nightclub

"These angry men planning a Straight Pride Parade [in Boston in 2019] just don't get it. They were never discriminated against, beaten up or killed for being straight. Their pride was never robbed from them… they never had to retrieve it… Angry and plum dumb."—**Chris Evans** (*The Avengers*)

"Straight pride is an oxymoron. Pride in what? In being so much more numerous that they could create and still largely maintain the anti-gay dictatorship we've lived under for 2,000 years?… Bigoted straight men are pride-*stealers*—they stole it from us. But many of us have taken it back!"—**Thomas Fowler**, whose partner of 58 years, Bart Howard, composed the song "Fly Me to the Moon"

"Any country that doesn't allow its gay citizens rights equal to those of its non-gay citizens cannot accurately be called a democracy… Christopher Isherwood nailed it when he coined the phrase 'the heterosexual dictatorship.'"—comedian **Bob Smith**

"The heterosexual majority has always demanded a 100-percent monopoly. Historically, our three Western religions have practiced the opposite of live and let live. Only in recent decades has this begun to change, thanks to a few people here, there and everywhere opening their mouths to challenge the socio-political-religious dictatorships we live under."—gay British actor-writer **Stephen Fry**

"As recently as this year's [2019] Academy Awards, in the car on the way to [the ceremonies] with my client Regina King, who won her Oscar hours later, I felt ashamed to drive down Hollywood Boulevard and observe ignorant and bigoted protesters holding up degrading signs painted with anti-gay and homophobic slurs.

"We have made progress over the past 20 years, but until LGBTQ people can feel pride without prejudice, there is significant work left to do."
—founding partner and ICM talent agent **Chuck James** in an op-ed piece titled "Pride Without Prejudice"

"It's time to live and let love."—**Lynn Redgrave**, daughter of a closeted gay actor

About the Author

Boze Hadleigh is the author of 26 mostly showbiz books. The *Los Angeles Times* dubbed him "a pop culture phenomenon." Hadleigh holds a master's degree in journalism, speaks five languages, has visited over 60 countries and won on *Jeopardy!* He is based in Beverly Hills, San Francisco and Sydney.

Other Riverdale Avenue Books You Might Enjoy

Hollywood Lesbians: From Garbo to Foster
By Boze Hadleigh

Hollywood Gays: Conversations with Cary Grant, Anthony Perkins, Liberace, Ceaser Romero and Others
By Boze Hadleigh

Deeply Superficial: Noel Coward, Marlene Dietrich and Me
By Michael Menzies

Wasn't Tomorrow Wonderful?
By Kenneth Walsh

50 Shades of Gay
By Jeffery Self

Valley of the Dudes
By Ryan Field

Also by Boze Hadleigh

Marilyn Forever
Elizabeth Taylor: Tribute to a Legend
Celebrity Feuds!
Broadway Babylon
Life's a Pooch
Holy Cow!
An Actor Succeeds
Elvis Through the Ages

Made in United States
North Haven, CT
27 December 2022

30103523R00114